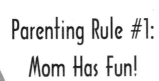

Parenting Rule #1: Mom Has Fun!

A Guide to Responsive Parenting

"Every Person Is Born a Genius"

Buckminster Fuller

Parenting Rule #1: Mom Has Fun!

A Guide to Responsive Parenting

Nicole Iselin MacKenzie

Skyward Publishing

Copyright 2002 by Skyward Publishing, Inc.

Publisher: Skyward Publishing, Inc.

    Phone: (573) 717- 1040

    Fax: (413) 702- 5141

    E-mail: skyward@sheltonbbs.com

    Website: www.skywardpublishing.com

Library of Congress Cataloging-in-Publication Data

MacKenzie, Nicole Iselin, 1958-
    parenting rule #1: Mom has fun!: a guide to responsible parenting / Nicole Iselin MacKenzie.
    p.cm.
    1. Parenting. 2. Child rearing. 3. Parenting and child. I. Title: Parenting rule #1: Mom has fun!. II. Title: Mom has fun!. Title.

HQ755.8 .M32 2002
649'.1--dc21

2001049438

To my children
Mia, Micah, Ian, Naomi
Ami, and Lydia
and all the children of
the world

Foreword by Dr. P. L. Mackenzie

Last year, at one hundred and two years old, my maternal grandmother passed away.

When we sat down to tell our kids, aged four to twelve, we tried to imagine what it was like when great grandmother was their age. They had no real concept of the way life might have been. We pointed out that not only was there no electricity (therefore to the kids amazement no Game Boys, Play station or TV) but that great grandma had to go outside to use the bathroom.

My children have been fortunate to fly a lot, all of them when they were very young. It was hard for them to even imagine not having airplanes or cars and other modern day modes of travel. This does not even take into account all of those other modern conveniences.

Peter Drucker, author of *In Search of Excellence*, says that the new millennium will be known not as the information or technology age but for the incredible number of choices that are available. He says the average 45-year-old man in our society is fairly sure he will not retire from the job he currently is in. To make matters worse, many of us, including our children, believe that they (our children) were not put here to work. If you don't believe this statement to be true, ask the parents of any teenager. With these combined facts, we have the setting for exactly what is happening in our society today.

The new millennium parents must address new issues: How do we raise our children to best prepare them for this fast changing world? What should be their criteria of success? When do we as parents do a good job? Where do you want your child to excel? Should the child excel in math, language, art, music, sports, medicine, law or in all of the above? When do you push them and when do you back off? How much can you expect of a child? How much responsibility can you hand them? How much freedom do you have to give them, and what is really your role as a parent? Should you be a guide, an authority figure, a friend, an enemy, a judge and jury, a jerk?

In our advanced technological society, our children have more opportunity in education and life than any previous generation. Shortly after Mia, our first baby, was born Nicole, Mia and I went to Philadelphia to 'The Better Baby Institute'. The exhibitions by the children were wonderful, and they showed many things that before this time I did not know were possible.

On one particular afternoon, after some of the resident students had finished a presentation, I had the great honor to walk out with Glen Doman, the founder of this innovative institute. As we stood together for a few moments, he said with a certain amount of pride and a tremendous amount of curiosity, "Wow, Doctor MacKenzie. Can you imagine what will be possible for children educated like this?"

Looking at him momentarily, I said, "No sir, I don't think I can."

"I guess I really cannot either," he added, laughing.

Our children (and we as adults) are being bombarded by choices and have no real standard for what is really important or valued in our lives. Most children today are the second or third generation growing up in a world where the first step to Self Actualization is a reality for most people. Their physiological needs are being met. They have a roof over their heads, a bed to sleep in, and do not, for the most part, wonder if they are going to eat. In fact, they generally are allowed to be picky about foods they eat and often can choose when they want to eat. In some respects, they have more understanding of life than we do. For example, a few years ago Nicole and I were arguing. She angrily retreated to the bedroom as I stomped to my retreat, the white throne. Mia, our oldest, was about four years old, and I heard her go upstairs to our bedroom. After a short time, she came back down the stairs. A few seconds later, she opened the door to my bathroom retreat and asked me, pretty much face to face: "What are you guys doing?"

I told her that we had a difference of opinion. She said, "I don't know why you guys do this. What it all gets down to is it is all about God anyway."

I asked her to repeat her statement, and she said, "When everything gets down to where it belongs, it is about God." You are mad and Mom is mad. Why do you do this?" I asked her to look at me. She did and said, "You are not mad." I said, "How could I be when you tell me such a truth." As one of my patients said years ago, "God does not have to hit me in the head too many times."

When babies are born, they are unconsciously Self-Actualized, unconditionally enlightened, if you will. Nicole shows you how, in her book, through enculturation that they (we) fall from this state of grace. So, let's look at the role models; let's look at adults. What makes adults happy? When are they satisfied? When do they have fun? These questions up until a few years ago were irrelevant. People were too busy surviving to wonder if they were happy or not. Up until now, most have looked outside themselves to determine success. Many of the baby boomers have found this shallow and incomplete.

I became a doctor, partially because my family wanted a doctor, and to me doctors seemed to live a better life than most people, at least monetarily. So, I became a chiropractor. I did not realize that every day most of the people I would meet would complain about something. I had been in private practice for about eight years when I walked out in frustration, depression, and confusion. I was trapped and had no notion as to what to do to change this situation. I had reached the top of the ladder of success and didn't particularly like my position on it.

Maslow researched the state of self-actualization and found that only a very small percentage of adults live in a state of self-actualization. Some get there seemingly by accident, some in old age, and others through surviving a tragedy (an idea well depicted in the movie "Fearless"). Everybody else pretty much lives a life motivated by emotions with the main attention on oneself, constantly in reaction and judgment and, therefore, only seldom happy and satisfied.

Daniel Goleman in *Emotional Intelligence* quotes the sixteenth century humanist Erasmus of Rotterdam's who says that "emotional thinking can be 24 times more powerful than the rational thinking." This sixteenth century quote may still hold a fair amount of truth for today's society. Although the world has changed drastically, as people our emotional evolution has stood rather still. However, when adults fulfill their passions, their true calling, find their gifts, they, during those moments, enter a state of complete satisfaction without worries or cares. When individuals step back into their personal lives, their emotions once again take control. This pattern can specially be observed in artists, actors, and successful professionals who truly believe in what they are doing.

The curiosity that needs to be in place if we are to raise happy children, therefore, lies in giving them cues as to how to continually find and sustain their own highest self (if you will) on one hand and develop their emotional intelligence on the other.

Parenting Rule #1: Mom Has Fun, a Guide to Responsive Parenting is designed to develop a child's emotional intelligence. The nonjudgmental feedback system, based on curiosity, not only improves a child's self-esteem, but it also allows them to share their genius and their most enjoyable persona. If parents apply these methods, the child will automatically develop strong emotional intelligence and, therefore, have a much better start toward a fulfilling life.

Nicole refers many of her clients to my class, Self Actualization - The Experience. These have so far been my best clients. People who know that they could be happier and who accept the truth that their children will "Do as I do, not as I say," are, to say the least, very strongly motivated.

Fourteen years ago I had the great good fortune to have my entire world turned upside down when I was introduced to the Sage Learning Method and allowed to experience my own Self-Actualization. Nicole's quest through the book and through her consulting has focused on helping parents keep their children in a natural state of Self-Actualization. The important question remains. Can we as parents assist our children in resisting the enculturation of society and see how life really is? And, can we assist children in consciously acknowledging the learned emotional states that rule and destroy so many lives.

I know it is possible, for I have witnessed it in our children and in Martin Sage's children. These children are asked to assume personal responsibility for their own fun and happiness. If this is your first introduction to the new learning method, you will find it easy and fun. Many people who have taken Nicole's classes have called her "the next Maria Montessori."

Table of Contents

Acknowledgments

First of all I would like to acknowledge my husband Mick. Without his constant push toward a life of curiosity, I most likely would have done things the old-fashioned way. I thank my children Mia, Micah, Ian, Naomi, Ami, and Lydia, for I never would have researched this topic without them. They teach me day by day and test my tools over and over again. What would I do with out you guys!

Many others I would like to thank at this point, for without their support and input this book would not be possible. Namely, Martin and Gigi Sage, who educated me in the Sage Learning methods. My mentor Melody Pritchard taught me much about raising children. Melissa White worked with my children and I for years. Tamara Balis assisted in developing some of the tools mentioned in this book while teaching in our school. Amy Sheesly helped me write the "game-part" of the book. Diana Rittinger, Beverly Benthal, Roberto Sciffo, and Aline Tatom helped with editing. Bernard Zick supported me, and my mom taught me the basics of "fun" parenting.

Introduction

Responsive Parenting is a step-by-step guide to raising children in a way that nurtures their unique potential while having fun. In the following pages, you'll read about discipline without punishment, you'll learn to make distinctions without criticism, and you'll find out how to hold your child totally accountable to his or her potential. You'll also learn *Rule #1: Mom and Dad Have Fun.* I believe that having fun is one of the basic requirements for doing a good job as a parent.

As a new parent, holding your newborn baby for the first time, you want to raise that child in a way that will nurture its unique and individual genius. Unfortunately, somewhere along the way, parents focus so much on the everyday challenges of parenting that they fail to see the genius in their children. They end up constantly correcting misbehavior which is not much fun and can bring up feelings of anger, resentment and, eventually, guilt.

Responsive Parenting is a revolutionary new way of parenting. It not only nurtures your child's genius but also builds the child's self-esteem, level of responsibility, and level of fun. And, best of all, it increases the level of fun you have as a parent.

Some of the key questions of parenthood are as follows:
• How do you raise children in a way that nurtures their unique potential and stay sane?
• How do you hold them accountable to their potential?
• How do you raise confident, respectful, self-reliant, responsible, and cooperative children who contribute to society?

Given the right structure, children will flourish naturally. The parent's job is to provide that structure and consistency and to hold children accountable for being the best they can be. At the same time, parents also need effective tools to deal with misbehavior.

This step-by–step guide shows you how to build this structure and will give you the tools you need to raise happy, healthy children while having fun doing it.

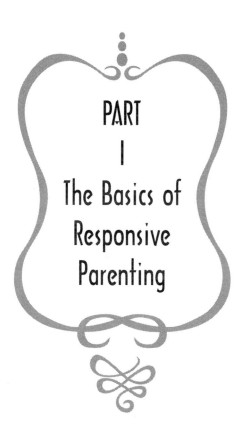

PART

I

The Basics of
Responsive
Parenting

Every Child Is Born a Genius

"Every person is born a genius;
– Buckminster Fuller

The curiosity is how to keep that genius alive, and how to raise children holding them accountable to their genius.

Each Child Has a Unique Genius

Every child is born with more genius than even Leonardo DaVinci ever exploited. Your child has a natural genius that if recognized and developed will provide a solid foundation toward a more fulfilling life. The purpose of *Parenting Rule #1: Mom Has Fun* is to show you as a parent how you can help your child develop natural gifts and abilities. The secret to the success of this program is that mom and dad have fun while engaging in helping their children grow.

Be Curious

Even though everyone is born with a natural gift, most, unfortunately, never develop or recognize that gift. Combining the curiosity of your child's actions with the right training and tools will bring to surface the genius within your child.

You may be thinking that "genius" is a term that applies only to special, rare, and those one-in-a-million people. In actuality, research shows us time and again that each one of us is born with nearly unlimited potential. For example, Glen Doman[1], founder of the Better Baby Institute, has dedicated his life to discovering how to tap into more of the human brain potential. One child came to him with physically half a brain. The child had been classified as mentally retarded. Doman worked with the child very intensely both mentally and physically for many years. This child eventually earned a college degree. Most of us are working with an entire brain. Imagine the possibilities!

And yet, using more of your brain's potential doesn't necessarily mean you are satisfied or happy. I believe that satisfaction in life is directly related to using your unique gift (more of your essence). Thus, the ultimate search is to find each child's unique gift, the child's passion. One child may be an artist by essence and another may delight in bookkeeping. If upon reaching adulthood, a child chooses a profession that honors that passion, the child's life will be much more fun and rewarding, and the child will be much more effective at the chosen job or profession.

Not a Candle but a flame

> *George Burns found what he loved to do early and saw his potential. Because he was willing to live the life he came here to live, he impacted hundreds of thousands of people, bringing joy and humor to their lives. He had a blast, and he was totally alive!*

[1] Glen Doman reference

> *George Bernard Shaw, the famous author and poet,*
> *lives his life not just to be a candle but to be a flame so*
> *bright he can light up the lives of many people. His drive*
> *to do what he was born to do has allowed him to contin-*
> *ue to touch the lives of many.*

There are many who have followed this wisdom. Among the known are Einstein, Mozart, Maria Montessori, Albert Schweitzer, and Pablo Picasso. Others, too, have developed their gift and passion and people continue to do so, even against the strains of society. These people rely on more than intelligence. Research points out that even Einstein used about 10% of his brain capacity, but Einstein used his gifts and believed in his abilities. Developing and nourishing his gifts made him like Shaw, a "flame" among his peers.

The world is changing at lightning speed. Since my grandmother's time, we've moved from the horse to the car to airplanes and on to putting a man on the moon. We now communicate in milliseconds instead of weeks. We don't know what it will take to be a successful adult in the new millennium. (What will be the successful careers in twenty years— X-games, teenage e-commerce millionaires, etc?) What we do know, though, is that if a child is allowed to follow individual passion, the chance for a more fulfilled, happy, and satisfied life is tremendously increased.

The Current Condition

When you as a new parent hold your newborn baby for the first time, you want and dream of ways to raise your child in such a way as to help this precious individual grow, flourish, and be successful in the future. Since the future is unpredictable, the child will be most flexible and adaptable when allowed to be happy and nurture individual talents and abilities.

Unfortunately, somewhere along the way, we as parents focus so much on the everyday challenges of parenting that we can develop myopic vision. While directing our attention on the day-to-day survival strategies, we may fail to see the genius in our children. We end up constantly correcting misbehavior rather then viewing each child as a unique person with unlimited abilities. Not only is this not much fun, but when merely surviving each day, our feelings of anger, resentment and, eventually, guilt rise to the surface and attack our energies. Negativity sets in and is transferred to our children.

Two Parents at Work

Two parental careers can incite another problem. Today's mom enjoys working outside the family unit to develop and enhance her life. While mothers should develop their talents and gifts, it leaves kids in daycare centers and schools for a large portion of the day. Many working parents feel guilty about not spending enough time with their children. To ease guilt, these parents tend to start spoiling their children more than they otherwise would.

A Disciplinarian I Will Not Be

Parents are responsible for providing disciplinarian duties, a sometimes difficult job. To further complicate the problem, there is a part of us that desires to shun this role. One reason could be that we are often unsure of the limits we should place on our children. "Should I give them the extra chocolate? They want it." Or, "Did they have enough?" And, what of today's social and official laws? Which ones do we agree or disagree with? As parents, we desire to give our children as much freedom as possible, but freedom without proper boundaries creates problems. Without discipline, children soon learn that they are in control and start to run the whole house their way. I have seen homes where a three-year old runs the entire household! A lack of discipline sets up an ironic situation that needs immediate attention. Without proper boundaries, parents fail to bring out the best in their children. Actually, the opposite happens, and children become dissatisfied, controlling, and whiny. They become more and more demanding, and eventually nothing will ever be good enough. Nothing will really satisfy them anymore.

So What Is a Parent to Do?

Some look to past disciplinarian practices to find answers. The wisdom of past generations of child rearing can collectively be useful, but the old system has many flaws. There was often a strict disciplinary system in which children had no rights and had to obey orders. Today, there is a better way, a way that reflects what we've learned in the twentieth century and fits with our vision for the next century; a way that treats each new being entrusted into our care with a tremendous amount of respect; a way that keeps that precious being's genius and vitality alive. And the implementation of this way comes from curious parents—parents who "get curious and stay curious" until the challenges are resolved.

Responsive Parenting

Responsive Parenting is a revolutionary new way of parenting. It is a handbook and guide that shows how to raise children in a way that nurtures a child's unique potential while keeping you, the parent, sane. When you nurture your child's genius, you build self-esteem, ingrain responsibility, and allow for a level of fun that includes fun for the parent and the child.

In the following pages, you'll read about discipline without punishment, you'll learn to make distinctions *without* criticism, and you'll discover how to hold your child *totally accountable* to his potential. You'll also learn *Rule #1: Mom and Dad Have Fun.* Just as at work, in parenthood, or in anything else, without fun, one is less productive and less energetic to do a good job. I believe that having fun is one of the basic requirements for doing a good job as a parent.

Let's Get Started

First take a moment to relax and congratulate yourself for doing a great job so far with your children because if you have even the slightest bit of curiosity about this book, you are doing a great job! You are actually doing the one thing that will make all the difference— *you are curious.*

My whole approach to parenting is based on curiosity. So, as you're reading this book, stay curious, and most importantly—*have fun with this book!*

This is not a rigid guide on how to handle each step; it is rather a helpful toolkit to be used with lots of curiosity on the parents' part. Try different tools and see what works for you, but always stay curious.

Kids Need Boundaries

So, how do you raise children in a way that nurtures the child's unique potential while you as the parent have fun? How do you hold them accountable to their fullest potential? How do you raise confident, respectful, self-reliant, responsible, and cooperative children who contribute to society.

Given the right structure, children will flourish naturally. The parent's job is to provide that structure and consistency and to hold kids accountable to performing their best. Best here does not mean that you set your standards according to societies rules but that you establish what is best for your child's potential. At the same time, parents need effective tools to deal with misbehavior.

Kids Need Boundaries and Consistency

In our desire to give our kids everything we think they need, we sometimes fail to give them boundaries and to set limits to their behavior. We don't want to be unreasonable and limit or deprive them.

Paradoxically, setting boundaries actually creates more freedom for children. It clearly outlines what is acceptable and unacceptable behavior. They know that as long as they stay within specified boundaries, they're Okay. And, they know that the minute they step outside those boundaries, they're misbehaving and will be disciplined. This disciplinary policy allows children to control their behavior. Children need parents who set rules and implement proper consequences when those rules are broken. When you're consistent, your children know you can be trusted to hold them accountable.

The Opposite Is Also True

If you fail to set boundaries, your children have little, if any, way of knowing what's considered acceptable behavior and what isn't. They live in a state of uncertainty, constantly testing the limits. You end up having to repeatedly correct and nag. They soon tune you out and don't listen to you. Under such circumstances, everyone is frustrated, and the situation deteriorates from there.

The Boundary Exercise

This exercise will give you an experience of how boundaries work. Only turn one page at a time! (No cheating or looking ahead.)

Turn to the next page and circle the numbers in sequence (1, 2, 3, 4, 5, 6, 7, 8 ...etc.) *as fast as you can.* You have *two* minutes. Then, turn to the next page.

Boundaries Exercise Part I

```
1    41      85              30      98  90
    9       21      53           10  14  86
61                         42      94
77  5   25      37      58
        13  81      89  78   6   22   62
   93  17           65          82      50   66
57  33  29  45      69  54  26  18   2    38
    73  97  49          34      70      46      74
91              55      12  32      52   64
    15  31          51   8   56      44
    7       23              60
27  43  59      63   36      20              100
    95      71   35  80      28      96
11      19   47          40  16              24
    39  67  83   3   68   72          92
87   99   79   75          76  88   4   84  48
```

How many did you get? Was it easy? What emotions did the exercise bring up?

Often people think that this exercise is quite frustrating, since you have to look for a certain number for a long time. It is not easy to shine and a certain pressure of failure is often felt. "Can't see the forest for all the trees!"

Evaluate yourself. *Did you feel competent while doing the exercise or rather overwhelmed?*

Part Two

This time, I will give you more instructions and smaller boundaries:

1. Once again, you have *two* minutes to circle as many numbers as possible in sequence.

2. The first number will be in the *upper left* hand square; the *second* number will be in the *upper right*-hand square; the *third* number will be in the *lower left*-hand square; the *fourth* number will be in the *lower right*-hand square, and so on.

3. Turn the page and start now.

Boundaries Exercise Part II

```
1    41      85        |    30      98 90
    9      21      53  |       10  14 86
61                     |    42      94
77 5   25    37        | 58
     13   81      89   | 78  6   22    62
93  17           65    |    82      50   66
57 33 29 45      69    | 54 26  18  2   38
   73   97   49        | 34    70    46    74
-----------------------+-----------------------
91            55       | 12  32    52    64
   15 31          51   | 8    56       44
7        23            |    60
27   43  59      63    | 36     20          100
    95      71   35    | 80    28   96
11     19    47        | 40  16            24
   39 67 83    3       | 68  72        92
87    99  79   75      |    76  88 4   84 48
```

How was that? How many did you get this time? How did you feel this time? Did you feel more self-confident?

Having more precise instructions, having smaller boundaries, and knowing the rules (the pattern) made it easier to find the numbers didn't it? With boundaries, you probably felt more confident and felt you had an attainable goal. The boundaries made it much easier to do a good job, and that, in general, makes people feel more satisfied.

When children have precise rules and smaller boundaries, they experience that same sense of relief and ease. Boundaries really do work.

Kids Will Test the Boundaries

- It's their job to test you to see if the boundaries really hold up.

- It's your job to be consistent and hold them accountable immediately when they step outside the boundaries.

Holding your children immediately accountable is the only way they will know that the boundaries are real and fully understand that you will keep your word. If you don't hold them accountable to the boundaries you set, they will step further and further over them. When that happens, they soon lose trust in your word.

Example

❧ ❧ ❧ ❧ ❧

When flying with my children from Switzerland to the United States, we usually have one long flight and then a layover in Chicago. After an eight-hour flight, the kids are full of energy and need physical movement. I find a calmer area of the airport for them to play and set down imaginary boundaries for them.

I verbally give them instructions such as: "The boundaries are from the door to this chair to that post to the wall." Within those boundaries, they are free to run, chase each other, and so fourth. The minute they step outside the boundaries, they look at me to see if I will hold them accountable. If I don't say anything, they step farther and farther outside the boundaries until pretty soon they're running all over the airport. If, on the other hand, I hold them accountable the instant they step outside the boundaries and give them a timeout, they soon stop testing, relax, and freely play.

Accountability and Discipline

Boundaries clearly communicate to children what is acceptable and unacceptable behavior. Children are responsible to their caretakers, and since the caretakers are the ones "In-Charge," providing children with appropriate boundaries will encourage harmony and avoid disharmony.

Discipline is simply what happens when a child steps over those boundaries? This follow up action shows children that we as adults are serious about the boundaries we set.

Keep in mind that the objective here is not to gain domination over subordinate children whose behavior we find irritating and disruptive. The objective of discipline is to enforce boundaries so children learn to respect them. In order for discipline to build a child's self-respect and self-esteem rather than destroy it, the discipline needs to come from a place of profound respect and appreciation.

Respect and Appreciation

Children are our equals and are entrusted into our care. To build a foundation for self-esteem to take root and grow, communications between family members, even those involving discipline, need to reveal that disciplinary actions are not punishments but are provided so all will appreciate and respect one another. Adults respect children and children in turn respect adults.

Because we are older and wiser, we happen to be "In-Charge". That means we're also responsible for teaching our children basic patterns of behavior. It is our responsibility to show our children, by example, how to treat others with respect and appreciation. Children learn by imitation. They copy adults. If your approach is one of respect and appreciation, they will more than likely copy that behavior and will not only respect you but will also respect others as well.

Treating others with respect and appreciation also builds self-respect and self-esteem. The more we appreciate and respect others, the more we can appreciate and respect ourselves. The more we appreciate and respect ourselves, the more we can appreciate and respect others. It will be easier for children to learn self-respect and self-esteem if they're around adults who themselves have a profound appreciation for life.

Isn't Misbehavior a Sign of Disrespect? Absolutely not. At the root of most misbehavior is a search for power. It's a very sophisticated "game" the child is playing to see if your buttons can be pushed. The game is played solely for the sake of a possible win.

Instead of getting mad and being pulled into the power struggle, appreciate and admire the brilliance of their game. Then, hold them accountable.

What If I Get Pulled into the Power Struggle? When your kids are misbehaving and you find yourself drawn into a power struggle, it's probably because you've become emotionally engaged. This is something many parents deal with on a daily basis.

Most good parenting books suggest that you should avoid getting emotionally engaged when your kids misbehave because when emotionally involved, you cannot effectively discipline your children or hold them accountable for misbehavior. Emotional engagement leads to disciplinary punishment as the action is out of reaction. Such an inter-action will usually result in a counter-reaction in the child and probably some guilt in you.

If, for example, you are in a store with expensive ceramics and your three year old daughter is completely fascinated by the exposition, the odds are she will touch everything. You tell her calmly: "Mary, don't touch any-thing in here!" But, of course Mary can't help herself, and you keep on catching her touching the ceramics. Three more times you tell her not to touch, and by the fourth time you're engaged emotionally. Now, you are yelling at her. You are mad, not because she is touching the ceramics but because she is disobeying you; she must be disobeying because she keeps ignoring your order. It is now personal. You are engaged in a power-struggle, and you will react!

Punishment is guaranteed when you, the parent, get emotionally engaged.

4

Emotional Engagement Leads to Punishment

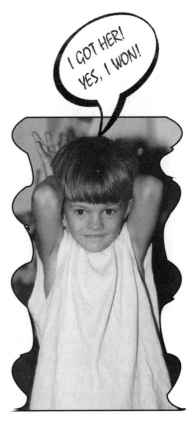

When you are emotionally engaged in a situation with your child, you are caught up in a power struggle.Emotional engagement is a state of mind where one loses sight of the whole picture and focuses directly on the 'situation' looking for a cause— someone to blame. It is now personal. You are right, and "they" are wrong. And, you will do whatever it takes to prove it to them, and you will win the fight. You will have no mercy. You are judge and jury. Here is an example on how your thought process might work:

Someone did something wrong.
I got personally offended.
That person is wrong.
That person is bad.
I am right.
I must provide punishment.
It must hurt, since only then is justice served.
The person will mind me.

In fact, when you're emotionally engaged, *any*
communication, in action or otherwise, is punishment.

---

*One day when my oldest daughter was seven years
old, she tried to push my buttons. Because she was upset
with me, she took a pen and wrote all over my leather car
seats. When I caught her, I was furious. She was so
wrong! I was personally offended, and I was going to
make her mind me. I was caught in her trap. I was emotionally engaged!*

*At the time, one of my mentors, Melody, was our
nanny. Melody saw what was happening and very calmly said to me, " Nicole, you are completely engaged. I'll
handle it!" I was still furious, but I was relieved to turn
the situation over to her. I knew from experience that I
would have punished Mia and would have later felt
guilty. Melody was able to hold Mia accountable without
making her feel as if she did something wrong. Melody
had Mia clean up the mess. It took hours.*

*Mia had only one purpose when she wrote on the car
seats. She wanted to engage me in a power struggle. She
almost had me, but thanks to Melody's intervention, I
was able to detach myself from the situation. Once she
found out she wouldn't get the desired effect, she never
did it again.*

Let me add that there is no way to fake your feeling if you are emotionally engaged. If you try to keep things light and friendly, the kids will see right through you. On the other hand, it is possible to really yell at your kids to get their attention without being emotionally engaged. The difference is that you are not yelling automatically. You are choosing to yell to get a desired effect.

When you allow yourself to get emotionally engaged in any situation, guess who will always win. Regardless of the punishment you devise, the other side wins the minute you react to the situation. Be it kids or adults, the other side wins the emotional game.

The Alternative: Responsive Parenting

If you want to have a good life, make everyone around you right.
If you want to have a great life
make everyone around you and yourself right!

What is a parent to do when children overstep the boundaries? You observe and respond. It is not necessary to scold or punish behaviors that we consider inappropriate. It is best to approach each situation with a detached clear view of the facts, without any emotional engagement. Children aren't wrong for what they do. They just failed to respect the boundaries and need to be held accountable for their actions.

Observation without Judgment

The alternative to emotional engagement is observation without judgment. Observation without judgment is the key to a successful and happy environment. Think of it as a spectator watching a movie. The spectator does not get personally involved or emotionally engaged in the action. A spectator stays detached from situations on the screen. Spectators have no agenda nor any point to prove.

When you stay personally detached from a situation with your kids, you can observe what's going on without judgment. The kids are not right or wrong. They are not good or bad. They are simply acting out a situation, and you are just observing what's going on. It's not personal. It's not about them being wrong or you being right, and it's not about you proving to them that they're wrong or bad and that you're right. It's simply about the inappropriate behavior that you have observed. You can then choose how to respond rather than *react* automatically. This type of behavior is much less stressful for everyone involved.

> *Ami, my second youngest, wants some gum. I tell her, "No," and she starts whining and begs, "Please, Mom, please." Instead of getting emotionally engaged, I say: "Ami, I said no. It is firm. Now you're whining and negotiating. That doesn't work. Come here and sit down. Do your consequence." (A timeout.)*

When you observe your child misbehaving, it's best to respond *right away*, but make sure you are *not* emotionally engaged.

Response Versus Reaction

When you see a game designed to engage you emotionally, respect it for what it is. Appreciate your child's brilliance in coming up with such a sophisticated game to manipulate you and push your buttons. Admire the child's brilliance in figuring out how to do it. This thought process will also help you keep from getting engaged. Accept that your child's actions and reactions are not personal. You will then be in a much better position to respond to the misbehavior rather than reacting emotionally and ending up in a power struggle.

When kids attempt to engage you in a power struggle through inappropriate behavior and they don't succeed because you respond without making them feel wrong, the game changes into a *win-win situation*. They learn they *can* trust you to catch them at their games, and it is then easy to correct inappropriate actions.

The First Level of Response— Feedback

One of the best responses to inappropriate behavior is simply *clean* feedback. Feedback is simply telling the child what you are observing. Feedback helps the child become more aware of what they are doing that's inappropriate and helps them see the impact of their actions. It also lets them know that you know what's going on too.

You can only provide *clean* feedback when you are not emotionally engaged and when you keep from forming a judgment or taking a position concerning the particular situation. The child is not right or wrong; they simply did something inappropriate. They simply did something that didn't work.

Example

❧ ❧ ❧ ❧ ❧

It is easy to give immediate feedback to your child's friends. Then, it is less personal. Let's say the rule in your house is that everyone must remove his or her shoes before entering the house. Since the rule is said in a matter of fact manner, without judgment, most kids will accept the rule and follow the instructions. On the other hand, if it is your child who for the 200th time marches into the house with shoes on, it is a little bit harder to give feedback. At that point, you need to go to the next step, which is setting up consequences

❧ ❧ ❧ ❧ ❧

If a child asks for something in a whiny voice, the feedback could be, "You just used the whiny voice! Try again, but this time using your awesome voice!" Give the child feedback if you want the child to change. Help the child practice using the awesome voice. When the awesome voice comes through, tell the child how much you like that voice. The child will quickly get the message and will use the awesome voice when wanting something.

The Next Level of Response—Consequences

If the inappropriate behavior is significant enough, you can implement the consequence for that action. *Be careful!!!* Consequences are like feedback; they only work if you don't make your children feel they were wrong for a particular behavior. The minute a consequence is given in the spirit of "you are wrong" the consequence turns into a punishment. You really have to watch yourself here; this is why one cannot get engaged and must look at the situation as an observer and not as a participant.

Remember that children are *not* wrong for what they do; they just failed to respect the boundaries and, therefore, must be held *accountable*. Consequences for actions hold children accountable, and children who are taught accountability are well on their way toward becoming responsible adults.

If a child knows the boundaries in advance and is willing to take the risk and essentially chooses the consequence, *it is the child who chose the outcome*. All you have to do is respect the choice and follow through with the consequence. Don't get mad because your little Johnny or Sally Ann chose differently than you would have wanted. Accept it and move on.

There are three types of consequences – natural, agreed upon in advance, and decided on the spot.

Natural Consequences: With natural consequences, you simply let the world give the feedback. Only choose this solution when your child will be safe!

> *This example illustrates natural consequences. It is a cold winter day, and your four year old son wants to go outside. He doesn't want to put his gloves on. You say to him, "Look, I think it is very cold outside. You may need gloves. But, you can decide that for yourself. You are old enough! So, if you get cold just come back in and get your gloves." Most of the time, your son will make a smart choice, and he actually feels very good since he can decide for himself. Best of all, there is no power struggle!*

Consequences agreed upon in advance: In this situation, you agree with your child up front about the consequence for stepping over the boundaries. Make a list and hang it on the fridge. When my kids were younger, I made drawings next to the consequences so they could still read the list. Often a physical assignment works very well and may include things such as running around the house, running up the steps five times, or a cleaning assignment.

The goal of the consequence is not punishment. You are using consequences to shift a child's focus and attention. So, if the child is in a negative mood or has a bad attitude and you give a cleaning assignment, the focus on the assignment will help the child to detach from herself, and the child's mood will be lifted. You may hear stomping and slamming of doors when the child is sent to the bathroom to clean, but soon after you may very well hear whistling or humming.

> *Here is another example of a powerful way to use consequences to get the desired behavior you want from your child. Take the shoe example. First establish the rule: The rule of the house is that we take our shoes off outside!*
> *Now set up a consequence if the rule is not followed:*
>
> * *If you come in the house with your shoes on, you have to vacuum the entire house!*
> * *If the child enters the house with shoes on, immediately implement the consequences. What do you think will happen the next time the child enters the house? You bet! Those shoes will be left outside the door.*

It is important to frequently update the list of consequences. Adjust them every other week.

Consequences decided on the spot: It is tough to stay disengaged when you have a new situation and you have to make up a consequence on the spot. Regardless, remember that these consequences, like the others, will only work if you're not emotionally engaged. Once established, these consequences will work best if applied from that moment forward and not for the event that initiated the consequence. However, in some cases, they need to apply right away in order to get the child's attention.

> *When one of my sons was five years old, we found him swinging our puppy around by his leash. He was showing his friend how well the puppy could fly. After freeing the scared puppy, I explained to him why flying a puppy is not in the best interest of the puppy nor is it acceptable behavior. Then, I had to come up with a consequence on the spot. He lost all his rights to be with the puppy for a week. It seemed like forever to him, and he was upset. I think that was the longest week in his life. After one week, he could only be with the puppy in the presence of a grown up. He had to prove that he could be trusted to treat the puppy with respect. This consequence worked very well.*

"What Do I Do When I'm Mad?"

We all have those times when we are completely engaged. We just know that our child did something very wrong, and we *have* to provide some kind of punishment. At that moment, we're willing to do whatever it takes to make the child mind.

Believe me, I have been in this position numerous times, and I have yet to meet a parent who *always* stays calm. When mad, I tell my kids, "I am mad. I need to take a break." Then, I take a break to blow off steam until I can talk without too much anger. The first thing I do when I come back is call a team meeting. A team meeting means that everyone stops all activities and joins together as team. These meetings not only bring families together so they can function as a team, but they also provide valuable time for anger to subside. For the meeting, everybody 'checks in with' (expresses) one thing that *personally* worked well and one thing that that didn't work. (*see page 90*)

Next, I take a few moments to look at the situation. Most likely, I'm able to look at it with more detachment, get "curious" about it, and make a better decision about how to handle it. If appropriate, I can then handle the misbehavior by implementing a consequence.

One day, I took my five children to a birthday party. For some reason, after leaving the party, I was angry. We went to a grocery store on the way home, and they were behaving well. But, I was so mad that nothing they did was good enough. They couldn't walk right or even talk right. I stopped in the middle of the store and said, "I need to have a team meeting." We held the meeting and then I said, "I am sorry. I am really mad right now, but it has nothing to do with you. I know that, so just stay out of it." They were very understanding. I felt a lot better. They felt a lot better, and we came together as a team, really looking out for each other.

On another occasion, Micah wanted me to help him with his homework. After assisting him and making sure he understood the concepts presented to him, I wanted him to work on his own. He started to whine, saying, "Mom, I can't do it. I don't know what to do. Please, Mom, help me."

Even though I could clearly see that he was playing a game, I started to get engaged. I started to react, which just made him whine more. Mia, my oldest daughter was watching the whole scene and came over to me and said, " I think we need a team meeting."

Frustrated, I called a team meeting. It worked! After I acknowledged that Micah got me completely engaged, and he acknowledged his whining, we both felt better. He then finished his homework without asking for additional help.

"What Do I Do When My Emotions Take Over, and I React?"

Since we are all humans, emotional reactions can occur quite frequently. Remember that it is all right to make mistakes! In this situation, I allow myself time to calm down and call a team meeting. After the team meeting, I acknowledge my mistake and apologize for getting emotionally engaged. We all look at the situation and discuss how we are going to avoid it in the future.

6

Controlling the World of Emotions

Emotions vs Sensations
Fear vs Trust; Tiredness vs Passion; Anger vs Excitement;
Sadness vs Ecstasy; Anxiety/Enthusiasm;
Melancholy/Inspiration; Depression vs Bliss

Emotions are the *shadow* qualities of sensations.

There is a clear distinction between emotions and sensations. Emotions have been learned, are created by the mind and are the reflective feelings of sensations. For example, if we were to ask a one year old to be depressed or sad, the child wouldn't understand what we meant even if we explained it.

The importance of this distinction is that it is the emotions that 'engage' us in a situation with our children, and emotions are also the reason why our children are able to play manipulation games with us(because we RE-ACT).

Emotions are, in essence, not bad as they play an important role in our communication within society. We can't avoid emotions, nor would we want to. Emotions are the spice of life. So, I am not saying you should avoid teaching your child emotions. That would be like saying you should avoid teaching your child to walk. The only thing I would like to draw attention to is the fact that most of us do not learn how to work with emotions. Emotions work us, and are very often overwhelming and a reason for suffering.

Whether we're aware of it or not, each of us has had to work very hard to learn how to use emotions, yet by the time we are adults, we are masters at using them to impact and often manipulate our environment. We're taught that emotions are real, and certainly when we're experiencing them, they feel very real. We're also taught that emotions just happen and that it's normal to get "stuck" in them. We believe that we can't control them and justify our emotions if we can find a reason for them. These beliefs simply aren't true. Emotions are creations of the mind, designed to manipulate us and our environment. They can only be sustained by the mind. If, for example, an emergency occurs that demands your full focus and attention, you will be able to completely forget about the feeling of sadness or anger. You will be able at that point, to be completely in the moment.

To use emotions to get what we want is a complete science in and of itself, and an important part of this parenting book.

However, with the right training, we can learn how to live by choosing our action, rather than RE-ACT out of emotions, and can then better decide when to use emotions as we need and desire them. Emotions need *not* rule us–it is possible for us to learn how to rule them. An example of a totally emotional-free state, known as the state of self-actualization, can be achieved instantaneously in the presence of a direct emergency. In this situation, the perceived emergency is so great that it shifts one from an emotional world to instantaneously living that moment; nothing else. This is to say that family influence, peer influence, cultural/religious influences and so fourth, have no role in the moment.

With regards to our children, they too learn to manipulate with emotions and unless they are made aware of this fact, the initial game of emotional manipulation can easily develop into an unconscious habit. The ability to recognize the emotional reaction will make their life much easier, happier and more energetic. This in turn allows their focus to shift to something other than themselves (e.g. my toys), and allows their genius to shine (e.g sharing my toys as it will be more fun).

Our job as parents is to learn how to deal with emotions more effectively. We need to learn more about them. We need to become aware of our emotions and of how we use them. We need to become conscious of the impact of our emotions on ourselves as well as others. We need to become more aware of our emotions and be "curious" about them. Then, we can learn to control them, rather than have them control us. Once we've mastered our emotions, it is our job to teach our kids how to handle their emotions so they will grow up happier and healthier.

Awareness Comes First

Emotions are only a choice *if* you are *aware* of being in an emotional state. Curiosity is a willingness to explore a situation and see it from various angles. It is important to be curious about your emotions in order to become aware of them and find ways in getting out of an emotional state. Just in being able to see emotions for what they are, noticing them when you feel them, and staying "curious" about them will make life a much less personal event and much easier to deal with, and sometimes this simple awareness of a situation or an emotion is the perfect fix for it.

Curiosity Frees You

I believe that we are meant to experience emotions, and once experienced, we should then let them leave our system. Unfortunately, in most of today's societies, we've learned to keep emotions inside like bubbles. We continually stuff them in when they surface through habit or to prove that we are 'tough'.

Typically, out of western habits, when something triggers an emotion, we find a good reason to justify it, instead of just being "curious" about it. Mentally we create reasons *why* we feel a certain way and, therefore, we feel we have justified the emotional state, so we allow it to exist.

I am sad because. . . I am mad because . . .

We formulate and use such reasons as an excuse to reinforce the emotion. Here are some of the mental dialogues that we use with ourselves:

There is something wrong . . .

• It must be me...

• It can't be me...

• It must be you...

• Nobody can see it but me. . .

• Therefore, I must punish you. . .

Only in the world of the mind is there a right and wrong! It is difficult to be curious when we are sure of the cause, but only when we are curious can we truly discover the problem. Curiosity leads to exploration and enlightens any situation. It is important to stay curious.

With Awareness and Curiosity Comes Choice

If emotions are made up (a product of the mind), then they can be turned on and off. We can go there or not. We can snap out of any emotion if we want to, which means we actually have a choice. Being angry or sad is actually a choice!

> *When I am very angry, I will direct my anger at someone really close to me like my husband. We then argue. An emergency occurs. Let's say one of the kids gets hurt from a fall. Immediately, I switch the anger off to handle the emergency. Focused on the present, the anger is gone.*

> *Once the emergency is handled, I can go back to the argument and turn the anger back on or leave it off. It took an emergency to shake me from my anger. The point here is that emotions can be turned on and turned off.*

You can test yourself with a similar example for any emotion, and you most likely will find that you can actually turn any emotions off in an emergency situation. Most of the time, however, when involved in a tense, negative emotion, you don't have an emergency to wake you up, and you get "stuck" in the emotion without realizing what is happening. It is easy to forget that there is a choice.

Give Children Control Over Their Emotional World

Since emotions are learned behavior, it is important to teach children how to explore and work with their emotions. Most babies are born uninhibited, free of judgment and criticism in a space of unconditional love. They later learn the illusory, man-made rules of our society. They learn what's proper and what's not proper— what's right and what's wrong. And they learn how to manipulate with emotions.

From the very first day of life, babies start on their emotional learning adventure. As tiny infants, they mirror the emotions of people around them. If the mother taking care of the child is cranky, the baby will be cranky. If the person taking care of the child is in a good mood, the baby will be in a good mood. It is almost as if the adult's emotions wash through the child. As a personal example, I remember when I used to take my baby to business meetings. The minute the meeting got rough for me, my child started crying.

Children Are Experts in Emotions

By the time a child is two and starts to develop an ego, the child is already an expert in emotions. Children learn early on that emotions carry power. They have learned to play games with emotions and learned how to use emotions to manipulate adults. Even at this early age, all children know what buttons to push with what grown-ups. Does this sound familiar?

Alienation
Anger • **Being the Victim**
Competition • **Defiance** • **Doubt** • **Frustration**
Inequality • **Lying** • **Negotiation** • **Opposition**
Pressure • **Self Pity** • **Whining…**

When children start to use emotions to get what they want, they really are playing a game. Children readily take calculated risks. Risks help them learn how far they can venture. Risks also help them firmly establish needed boundaries. The thrill of the game and the sensation of power provide the necessary stimuli for children, and they clearly feel it is worthwhile despite the possibility of punishment. They may not be aware of the emotional manipulation game until you point it out to them. When you bring awareness to the situation (without judgment), they readily understand the game, realizing they are using it to get what they want, which most of the time is power. Although it starts for most as a game, it can easily develop into a habit.

Playing emotional games doesn't bring out the best in children. It is so easy to get stuck in a mood or attitude. As adults it is important to give your children a great gift. Give them the tools they need to control their emotional world. Teach them to be curious about emotions. This is one of the most important gifts you can offer your children as they journey through life. It is truly a gift that stems from love.

Your goals:

- To teach children how to be aware of, and to understand, the world of emotions.

- To teach them how to use their emotions productively.

- To help them realize that they have a choice to use or not to use emotions.
- To provide feedback when they use emotions, without judgment.

- To hold them accountable for the emotional games they play.

- To help them see how their emotions impact those around them.

The World of Emotions and the Body Centers

The world of emotions has also been called the *world of the mind or the world of memory*. Carl Jung called it the *world of the shadow*.

As stated earlier, experience has shown me that every emotion is the shadow of a pure sensation:

- The shadow of trust is fear.

- The shadow of passion is tiredness.

- The shadow of excitement is anger.

- The shadow of ecstasy is sadness.

- The shadow of enthusiasm is anxiety.

- The shadow of inspiration is melancholy.

- The shadow of bliss is depression.

Each one of these sensations, and its shadow, the emotions, can be associated with one of the seven body-centers, known in the Eastern cultures as *chakras*.(See figure 1, page 60, 61).

Emotions Take Away a Person's Vitality—
Children Learn Emotions

Babies come into the world bright, alive and in total amazement. They are still completely connected to the source, or God-like energy, and have no image of themselves. They just exist in each moment, with no concept of time, good and bad, or of emotions such as sadness or anger. They are completely content and satisfied with their existence. They live in a state of "unconscious enlightenment," and later learn emotional reactions and how to take things personally. As they learn the world of emotions, their chakras start to close one by one and their aliveness (their "lights") start to dim. The dimming is not bad in any way. It is just a process we go through in life. Growing up means moving from living in a world of pure sensation to a world of the mind, a world filled and often directed by emotions.

7th Chakra/Bliss - During a child's first few weeks on the planet, the child is still connected to the God-like energy of the universe. Slowly, as the baby "learns" the way of the world, the child loses the connection to the universe and the state of bliss. The baby starts to move into the child's body more and slowly loses the "being one with everything."

6th Chakra/Inspiration - As the baby begins to distinguish itself from other people and objects, the baby sees itself as a separate unit; inspiration and innovation, (the 6th chakra) starts to dim.

5th Chakra/Enthusiasm - Usually between 1½ and 2½ years of age, a child starts to develop an ego, seeing itself as a separate body. They start to create and relate to the persona(ego) and that ego needs to prove he/she has power, too.

The Child in the Mirror

Have you ever watched a baby pass by a mirror? My daughter Ami could run back and forth in front of a mirror ten times and wave happily at her smiling face each time. Until the age of 1 1/2, she would never realize that the reflection in the mirror was her. She would never realize that she was the image in the mirror. When children develop an ego, they begin to hold a picture of themselves. They no longer see themselves anew each time they look in the mirror. They see themselves, and they begin to see a picture of themselves.

As parents, we hold a picture (in our mind) of our children. With this picture, we help to shape their picture of themselves, and they begin to see themselves as that persona. For example, we might say, "Oh, Pete has a temper just like his dad." From our image of Pete, he takes on the image of a child with a temper—just like dad. And, what do you know? When Pete looks at himself, his mental image tells him that he has a temper, so he plays the game and proves it over and over again.

Children Learn to Make Value Judgments

As children develop an ego, they also begin to make value judgments. As a baby, *there is no concept of good or bad.*

Never would a baby think, "They won't like me because I am too short and chubby." Instead there is a complete and total satisfaction in children until they see themselves as a separate unit (1-2 years old).

It isn't until children learn our value judgments that they begin to see themselves as pretty or ugly, good or bad. At this point in their life, their enthusiasm set dimmed a bit more.

4th Chakra/Ecstacy - The next chakra begins to dim as children learn that *love is conditional.* Mom loves you *if* you clean your room. Dad loves you *if* you are quiet in the store. At this age (1-1/2 to 2 yrs old), children are recognizing their own power and beginning to talk back and challenge their parents. Parents sometimes withhold love and affection when the child is not doing as the parents wish, reinforcing the concept of *conditional* love.

3rd Chakra/Excitement and Teamwork - The next center, *excitement and teamwork,* gets dimmed when children see poor examples of teamwork around them. Many parents tell their children to live happy lives and to respect each other while they themselves are modeling a life of compromise and frustration. When parents say one thing and do another, children have no real example of teamwork. The challenge is to demonstrate teamwork by creating a relationship where you really enhance each other and bring out each other's full potential.

2nd Chakra/Passion - The next center, *passion,* gets dimmed during adolescence. Puberty hits, and the sexual juices kick in. However, it isn't safe for the total exploration of this sexuality and the repression dims the passion.

1st Chakra/Trust - This center shuts down when *we no longer trust ourselves* to live the life we were put on the planet to live and to contribute our own unique genius to the world.

Potential

World of Sensation & Experience

WONDER
VISION
CREATING VALUE
SHARING
POWER
INSTRUCT
RESPOND

FREEDOM
INTENTION
APPRECIATION
COMPASSION
AUTHORITY
MOVEMENT
CONNECT

INTEGRITY
PEAK EXPERIENCE
GENEROSITY
SELF ESTEEM
EQUALITY
SATISFIED
HONESTY

ALIGNMENT
CLARITY
COMMUNICATION
RESPONSIBILITY
COOPERATION
OBEDIENCE
FEEDBACK

CONDUCTIVITY
INNOVATION
WEALTH
MOMENTUM
TEAMWORK
PLEASURE
MONEY

AMAZEMENT
INTUITION
HARMONY
KINDNESS
BELONGING
SAFETY
SECURE

BLISS
INSPIRATION
ENTHUSIASM
ECSTASY
EXCITEMENT
PASSION
TRUST

Learned

World of Mind, Emotions & Memory

The Body's Seven Energy Centers (Chakras)	Core Seven Levels of Awareness	Core Seven levels of Mind	Seven Levels of Manipulation	Gardner's Eight Intelligences
Root/ Sensual	Trust	Fear	Deception/ Lying	Logical/ Mathematical
Innocence/ Sensual	Passion	Tiredness	Bargaining	Body/ Kinesthetic
Will/Power	Excitement	Anger	Pressure/ Inequality	Interpersonal
Heart/ Acceptance	Ecstasy	Sadness	Blame/ Conflict	Intrapersonal
Throat/ Speech	Enthusiasm	Anxiety	Whining/ Nagging	Verbal/ Linguistic
3rd Eye/ Clear/ Seeing	Inspiration	Melancholy	Not Listening/ Ignoring	Visual/ Spatial
Crown/ Transcendence	Bliss	Depression	Martyrdom	Musical/ Rhythmic

Emotions

The 1st body-center is located in the legs and is associated with the sensation of trust, and its shadow is fear. We feel the sensation of excitement, and it's shadow anger, in the 3rd body-center, located in our belly. There is a saying in German: "I have an anger in my belly!"

When, as a child, we learn emotions, we start to replace the pure sensations, experience in a certain part of the body with a more made-up mind and memory related or emotional based reaction.

For example, let's take a broken heart. Only in our mind can we create a broken heart; it has to be connected to a memory! If living in the now, as babies do, we cannot experience a broken heart. However, we will be able to experience love. Love is a pure sensation. They both will be felt in the same part of your body, the heart. Love is unconditional, yet a broken heart is created and sustained by memory and our mind.

Since we learn emotions, we can also learn how to develop the emotional intelligence in order to respond, versus merely reacting and taking everything personally.

This book demonstrates a brand new learning method designed to develop emotional intelligence. As a result, life will be taken much less personal and, therefore, impact us very differently.

As the child learns the shadow world of emotions, their lights of sensation dim. Let us now have a look at the emotions.

1st Chakra/Fear - The sensation babies are born with is trust - the emotion that affects this body-center is fear. Other emotions that stem from fear are: emergency, greed, punishment, denial, manipulation, and reaction.

Fear is a *learned* behavior! For example – your knees shake when your mind perceives a dangerous situation.

My twelve-year old daughter has been having periods where she experiences fear. These incidents occur more and more frequently and were not related to any incident. She calls it "Mr. Fear" visiting again. She mentally images us (her parents) dying or fears she will never see us again. We discuss this fear together with curiosity, and she knows to watch for the mind's tricks. The minute her mind tries to produce the fear or tries to convince her that the fear is real, she tries to find five more reasons why the fear exists. Understanding why something occurs often helps release some of the fear. Our daughter has found that to be true.

Remember that you can't avoid emotions, but staying curious about them helps you stay on top of them.

2nd Chakra/Tiredness - The emotions here are tiredness, dissatisfaction, danger, boredom, injury, repression, rigidity, punishment and guilt. Again, these are all *learned* states of being. Here is an example to illustrate this point. Have you ever heard a baby say, "I am so bored," or "I feel guilty," or "I am so tired?" or, "Just let me just push through this tiredness and finish this one job!" No. When a baby is tired, it goes to sleep. When Amy was about eight months old, she was playing in the floor, crawling around! She was very content, yet the next time I looked, she had stopped moving. I ran to check on her – she was sound asleep!

For older kids and adults tiredness can reflects a resistance to life! For example, your child may get really tired when having to clean his or her room, yet if a friend comes over to play ball, the child is full of energy

3rd Chakra/Anger - The 3rd chakra is also called the power center. Its essence is teamwork, power, and family. The emotions that affect the power center are anger, frustration, inequality, pressure, competition, control, and alienation. The emotions are always connected to blame. Someone else is doing something wrong; therefore, we have the right to punish them with our anger. Tantrums are often a result of anger in a child's system.

4th Chakra/Sadness - The sensation of this chakra is *ecstasy, compassion,* and *self-esteem.* The shadow is felt as sadness, self-pity, judgment, blame, helping, conflict, defiance, and not sharing.

Here is an example that shows a positive way to make children aware of their emotions. When Mia was seven years old she watched a movie one evening. I was not watching, but I could hear teenage kids playing all kinds of manipulating games in the movie. I even told Mia, who was fascinated with the movie, that I wanted to watch the movie with her one time and just see how many games we could detect. That night after giving her the usual hug and kiss, she called me back into her room with already a whiny voice and asked for another hug and kiss.

I responded from the kitchen table: "Not right now. I am doing something else!"

That was it. It blew her right into the emotion of self-pity. She started crying, yelling, "You don't love me anymore."

I could hear her complete involvement in the emotion, and I was curious about her reaction. I asked her to come to the table, which she reluctantly did. I took out my body chart and showed her where she was on an emotional level. Then, I started to help her understand the feeling that emotion created in her body. I asked her: "Where do you feel it? What shape does it have?"

She started to get somewhat curious and said it was black and round, sitting right in her heart area. I told her that I actually saw where she just learned about that emotion. I pointed out the scene in the movie she watched earlier, and I told her that she was just trying it on to see how it felt and to see the result it would create.

I then added, " Now here is how I look at it. You can have that emotion and go to bed, or you can snap out of it and go to bed. It will not really matter to me. All I want you to know is that you actually have a choice in what you do."

She looked at me with her big brown eyes and said, "Well, that was interesting." She gave me a big hug and happily went back to bed.

5th Chakra/Anxiety - This is the center for enthusiasm, appreciation, communication, and wealth. It is located at the throat and mouth area. Its shadow is anxiety, although parents know this center more as WHINING!! It is also connected to lying, cheating, deception, cheapness, arguing, nagging, pouting, sabotage, criticism, constriction, being a problem, and gossip.

6th Chakra/Melancholy – This center is located in your forehead and is associated with *inspiration, peak performance,* and *intention.* Its shadow is melancholy; hope, being a victim, dullness, opposition, habituation, pride, contempt, indecision, and failure to complete. Someone else is to blame for everything. One example is "hoping" to get a job done. If it is your intention to get a job done, you must take full responsibility and do whatever it takes to get it done. If you merely "hope" that the job gets done, it probably won't.

Quite a few mothers get caught in the emotion of being the victim. They sacrifice their lives and vitality for their families, and in doing so, they make everyone around them feel guilty.

7th Chakra/Depression - The last center of emotion on the chart is associated with depression, tyranny, acting nice, apathy, dullness, programming, quitting, and failure.

I have noticed that this kind of emotion often comes in the form of dullness and sets in around the third grade. In my research, I have found that it is not so much connected to age as to school pressure. Kids who aren't in school seem to be capable of hanging onto the belief that they can do anything. It also doesn't seem to depend that much on the teacher either. Even the best third grade teacher may lose quite a few kids in that realm of "Oh, I can't do anything right. I don't know. I don't care. I am a failure".

7

The Power of Belief

*The thing always happens
That you really believe in;
And the belief in a thing
Makes it happen.*

Frank Lloyd Wright

In truth, children are great human beings with very unique gifts. The greatest service you can give to your children is to see them, admire them, recognize their unique talent and believe in them. When you believe in your children, they will exhibit more talent, and the more you recognize and admire them, the more confident and responsible they will be. It is also important to hold your children accountable for whatever unique talents they display. They will then perform at their best.

Let Your Child out of the Box

Usually, when we first meet someone, we are open. We see everything they do without pre-judgment. As we get to know the person, we create a picture of the individual and proceed to hold that image in our mind. We actually see the person as well as the person's actions through a self-made filter rather than as the person actually might be. If we are not careful, our perception of others actually restricts their individual freedom. In our mind, we never allow them to grow or change. We lock them in our mental box.

We create these self-imposed images with everyone around us, including our partners. When we first meet our partner, we are in an "everything you do is right" emotional state of mind. When the person can't or doesn't live up to our created image (the "box"), we decide that the individual is "wrong" for failing to be who WE decided the person should be.

> *A public example of perception is President Ford. What does everyone remember most about President Ford? Most people remember that he was clumsy. Reality is different from perception here. President Ford was actually an extremely athletic person throughout school and played on varsity teams. Very early in his presidential career, he fell down, and the entire nation started to hold a picture of him as clumsy. Everyone saw him as being clumsy, and that's how he was treated. The picture created in people's minds soon became a reality.*

We Hold Pictures of Our Children

The pictures we create of our children are very powerful. They are influenced by the way we see them. If we "box" our daughter as "not good in school," we see her this way, and we *treat* her this way. Eventually she *becomes* this way. This "box" we placed her in becomes her self-fulfilling prophecy.

We reinforce the picture we have created by sharing our pictures with others. Parents do this all the time when they drop off their child with a new caregiver or other adult. We make remarks such as: "He is a picky eater." These comments are intended to prepare the new person for the image we have of our child, but the picture will also *automatically* influence how the new person *treats* the child. It takes away the child's freedom to be different from our mental picture. The child has no chance to make a fresh start.

> *If I hold a picture of my child Ian as a smart aleck, and if I tell another adult to be careful with Ian because he will talk back, that adult will immediately hold the same picture of Ian. Ian has no choice but to live up to this image and be a smart aleck, and thus the picture becomes stronger and more deeply ingrained.*

Children Hold Pictures of Each Other

Kids themselves quite often create and hold mental boxes of another child. For example, two girls may decide that a third girl who has red hair has a problem controlling her temper. The girls say, "We aren't going to play with her." If two children hold the same image, it becomes more powerful. As more and more children (and adults) buy into the picture, the red-headed girl does not stand a chance. She must throw temper tantrums as that is how she is seen and treated.

Free Your Child

If you could discard your mental boxes and look at your child fresh everyday, who would that child be? I am personally curious and challenge myself to look at my children with a clean slate everyday and not hold them to a mental picture. If I see Micah for who he is in every moment, I will never have to treat him like the whiny or incompetent kid he sometimes pretends to be. And he is able to move out of that box much more easily.

Be curious all the time. Your curiosity will help you discover ways to let your kids out of the mental "box" and will teach them to do the same for others.

Let Your Child out of the "Box"

Exercise

Child's Name: _____

What Kind of Picture Do You Hold of This Child?

You
Your Spouse
Grandparents
Friends

Create a 30-second Commercial

What do you want to say about your child? Observe your child and notice strengths. What is the child's genius? What do you really appreciate about this child? What do you most admire? This shouldn't be confining. How would you like a stranger to see your child?

Create a 30-second commercial about your child. Paint the picture showing your child's brilliance. Create a sentence you'll use to introduce your child.

Exercise

Child's Name: _____

What do you want people to know about your child?
The Commercial:

Now share the commercial with your child.

Commercials Can Open Eyes

I know a mother who once had lots of problems with her teenage daughter. They were consistently bickering, arguing, and fighting with one another. This mom made a commercial about her child and shared it with her child. Their entire relationship changed. The girl could not believe how much her mom actually appreciated her. This simple exercise got them both back on track and the commercial now hangs on the fridge as a reminder to everyone!

Here is the example of my commercial about my daughter Mia. Mia is a master in movement, rhythm, and music. She can watch a complicated new dance move once and then do it. She is extremely smart and very creative. She is loved wherever she goes. She is very trustworthy and outgoing. In short, she is the best thing that ever happened to me.

PART
II
What
to Do
Ahead of Time

8

Rule #1: Mom Has Fun

The first seven chapters have covered the theory and understanding of the challenges faced with raising responsive children; it is now time to cover the essence of *Parenting Rule #1: Mom Has Fun*. This will then be followed by a step-by-step plan for implementing fun and "Team Meetings" into your family. For clarity, I have divided this chapter into five main catagories:

8.1 RULE #1: MOM HAS FUN!

8.2 ONLY 1 ADULT "IN-CHARGE" AT A TIME

8.3 ESTABLISH THE RULES FOR YOUR SPACE

8.4 SET SPECIAL RULES FOR SPECIAL OCCASIONS

8.5 SAFETY FIRST

8.1 RULE #1: MOM HAS FUN!

> RULE #1
> MOM HAS FUN!

"What do you mean the parents are supposed to have fun? I thought we were supposed to make it fun for them!"

Anonymous parent

Believe me, I get this reaction a lot. My purpose in writing this book is to teach parents to have fun raising their kids. I believe it is the most important rule of all.

The Creation of a Martyr

Let's take a 'typical' realistic scenario.

You are single, and having fun. Then, you meet your mate. You love each other, and you get married. Now, you want nothing more than to have a child with your partner. Everything goes well, and you give birth to your first child.

Suddenly, the focus of your whole life changes. Life is not about you anymore. It is about the baby. At first, everything is perfect. You love that new being more than anyone you have ever loved in your life. You start to make many sacrifices for your baby.

As your baby gets older, the infant learns how to manipulate you with his or her emotions. The baby sees the power it has over this "big" person. Slowly, you become victimized by parenthood. Your kids are running your life. You have no life of your own, and you start to realize that something is wrong. You get progressively more and more unhappy about it, and you want to make sure that everyone in your family knows how stressed you are over the situation.

You become a martyr. You sacrifice your wants and needs for your children. Everything you do for them becomes a sacrifice. Even when you venture into what should be fun times, you suffer. For example, if your kids want to go to Disneyland and you don't, you take them and suffer the whole time. You sacrifice your wants and needs over your kids wants and needs over and over again. If the kids want to go to Chucky Cheese, you go there, even if you hate the place. You remind yourself that the kids have so much fun. The problem is that you, the adult, can't even remember how to have fun anymore.

Don't Sacrifice Yourself

Does that mean you should never do anything for your kids? Absolutely not! Just don't sacrifice yourself. Sacrificing yourself is a *mindset* that creates dissatisfaction in you, and worse, creates guilt and dissatisfaction *in your kids*. You can still take the kids to Disneyland or a Pokemon movie, but do it because you really want to. Do it for yourself, not just for them.

I have six kids, and we do a lot of kids' things. Whenever we do things that I know will be fun for me, we have a great time. When we do things just for them, I always seem to get aggravated sooner or later. Before the event is even half way over my inner dialogue begins with thoughts such as: Here I am doing something just for them, and they don't even appreciate it enough to behave!

Your Kids Want You to Be Happy

Kids are so refreshing to be around because it's so easy for them to have fun. However, they will enjoy themselves much more if you are having fun, too. So, the rule in my house is as follows: "Whoever is "In-Charge" of the kids has fun[1]."

Now, this is a two-way street. It is the kids' responsibility to make sure that I have fun. And, it's also my responsibility to have fun while being "In-Charge" of the kids. The interesting side-benefit to this rule is that your child's self-esteem actually increases by implementing this simple rule. Another benefit is that your child must get the attention off of him or herself in order to focus on you. The child becomes less egocentric and less likely to engage in personal emotions.

Fun for Everyone

If there are activities you would like your child to participate in and that you hate doing, find someone else to take your place for that event or activity. For example, I personally don't like or have fun going to Chucky Cheese. If I were to sacrifice my feeling and take the kids to Chucky Cheese, even though I hate it, I would unconsciously make sure that the kids get the message, and I would spoil their fun. To avoid spoiling their fun, I simply don't go. I find someone who loves to go there and ask that person to take the kids. This makes it a win-win situation. There is always a way to create a win-win situation, and it usually takes only a moment of rethinking to discover the answer.

Children Love to Make Sure You Have Fun

Looking out for you so you can have fun is a game for your children. *Children have one primary goal—to gain your attention and approval.* They also know that if you're having

[1]In our school, the No. 1 rule is "The teacher has fun."

fun, they are more than likely to get more attention and approval themselves. Don't sacrifice. Be demanding. Demand to have fun. If you are not having fun, stop everything and demand to have fun. The kids will soon learn to look out for you and make sure that you are having a good time.

Include Them in Your Fun

When you are doing something that is fun for you or that you really enjoy, include the kids, and most likely it will be fun for them, too.

Your children love to share your passion. They know that when you share your passion, you are sharing a very special part of you. So, whatever you are passionate about share it with your kids. You may open up that world for your child, too.

My mother is an artist, and while we kids were growing up, she opened up that world for my sister and me. We would hang out at art shows, helping her hang pictures and taking part in many crazy parties. It was a great experience, and I absolutely loved this side of my mother.

Often when my sister and I came home from school for lunch, we would find my mom in her studio, covered with paint. She would look at us blankly, wondering who we were. It would take her a few moments to get back into the 'real' world where she knew she had two daughters.

Looking at her watch, you could read the disbelief on her face. It was as if she were sure something was wrong with her watch. When working, she was so absorbed in her painting that she had lost track of time.

In a hurry my mother would fix a quick and simple lunch such as canned ravioli. Those lunches where always great because my mother was content and fun to be with, and the canned meal tasted better than something she could have made from scratch. By allowing herself to pursue her passion, my mother gave us a great gift—the gift of showing her children that she as an adult could actually do something that made her happy. In those moments, my mom was in a state of self-actualization. She showed me that if she could do it, it was also possible for me.

When It Just Isn't Fun Anymore

Whenever an event or activity stops being fun, I call a team meeting (see page 90). After we discuss the "what is working and what is not working" agenda, I let them know that it is no longer fun for me, and that as children they are not doing their job. Looking out for me and each other again takes the attention off them and brings the fun back. It's a great rule. You still can do everything you did before but with a different mindset.

If the team meeting doesn't bring the desired effect, I usually pack up the kids and leave. The outing was designed for fun. If it isn't fun, it should end. The advantage of this response is that it usually makes the next outing much more enjoyable.

What If Only One Kid Acts Up?

Often parents tell me that they don't think it is fair to interrupt everyone's fun just because one child acts up. Well, I have six children, and we stop many activities when one child misbehaves and pack up and leave for home. Even if the children are initially upset, by the time we arrive home, they're starting to have fun with some other activity.

One important lesson for the children to learn while growing up is "life is not fair - better get used to it." When the children learn that they function *as a team* and not *individually,* they soon find ways to keep each other in line when we go on family outings.

8.2 ONLY 1 ADULT "IN-CHARGE" AT A TIME

When an adult is "In-Charge", that adult is In-Charge of *everything*. If the child wants something, the child must go to the adult In-Charge. The standard answer from everyone else will be: "Go ask the one In-Charge." The adult who has taken on this responsibility at this time makes all decisions and sets the rules. It is fine for each parent to have separate rules; however, it usually works better if you agree on a few house rules.

Children on the whole are flexible and smart and easily learn how to adapt to different rules as long as they know whose rules apply.

> *Once we lived in a house by a lake. Since our Nanny lived with us, the kids had three adults in the house and three sets of slightly different rules, but the kids only had to follow one set of rules at a time.*
>
> *One adult took the children swimming every day. According to who took the children swimming, the kids had to respect different rules. With the Nanny, the kids had to stay in the shallow end, since that was what she was comfortable doing with them.*
>
> *With me, they were able to go out a little more, up to a specific point. With my husband, they could go quite a bit farther. When we all went to the lake together, the kids usually would ask if "Dad" could be "In-Charge." As long as their father had fun, he took charge, and his rules applied. When he needed some time for himself, someone else took over for him. The wonderful part about this was that the kids had fun no matter whose rule applied, as long as they knew the rules.*

8.3 ESTABLISH THE RULES FOR YOUR SPACE – PHYSICAL AND EMOTIONAL

You deserve to have your physical and emotional space. It is your space, and you pay the rent. Part of the fun of being a parent is that as long as the kids are in your space, you pick the rules as to how you want your space to be treated.

Establishing the rules will be different for each of us, so decide which rules will be important to you. Be realistic and consider others in the household and include those in with your personal wants and needs.

Disharmony can occur if mom and dad disagree on how to handle household space or can't agree on which rules are right or who gets his or her way? Does the person paying the rent make the rules? You and your spouse will have to decide such issues. While there can be some diversity in boundary rules, generally an established set of simple house rules will keep peace and harmony.

When the adults cannot agree, use this procedure to help bring about an agreement. Both adults should make a list of rules. Then, establish which rules enable both to best feel comfortable in the shared environment. There may be a little give and take since your goal here is to try to set boundaries that work for both adults. Some rules should be flexible and dependent upon who is "In-Charge". Finally, make sure the kids know who is "In-Charge", so they will know whose rules to follow when the adult "In-Charge" takes over. This prevents the kids from playing adults against one another.

My personal experiences show how rules vary from one person to another. One thing that annoys me is toys laying around the house. In the children's bedroom, the mess doesn't bother me as much. My friend, on the other hand, needs to have the kid's bedrooms picked up all the time. Her kids know and respect her rules. She must feel comfortable in her environment, or she will be unhappy and take it out on the kids. Kids would rather have mom and dad in a good mood. In a harmonious household, the kids have an easier time, and they are more relaxed.

This feeling at ease doesn't just concern physical space. As the adult, I can also decide what kind of emotional space I want to have. If I had a roommate who was angry all the time, I could throw her out, but you can't just toss out the kids when they feel tense or frustrated. You can, however, establish rules and boundaries for certain emotional behaviors and attitudes. One can start by following these guidelines:

1. Find a bit of quiet time. Sit down and write how you want your place to be kept.

2. Rate your rules, and pick out the five most important ones.

3. Call a two part meeting. Start with the team meeting and then move to a family meeting. A team meeting

is very short. You acknowledge one thing that worked and one thing that did not work. That is all. A family meeting is an open meeting with discussions, setting boundaries and consequences.

4. Without getting personally engaged, in a matter-of-fact manner, explain the five top priorities on how you want your space treated.

5. Have your family devise consequences for each rule that is violated. Be firm and let them know that if they can't pick one, you will.

6. Write the consequence next to the new rule.

7. Hang your list in a very visible and frequently visited place, such as the refrigerator door.

8. As soon as someone violates the list, have that person look up the consequence and implement it.

9. As soon as someone steps over the set boundary, this list will need to be replaced by a new one, handling new behavior.

NOTE:

It is important to start with only a few rules. It is better to have five and really implement them than five hundred and not act on them.

8.4 SET SPECIAL RULES FOR SPECIAL OCCASIONS

When we go anywhere, we set the rules of the day by verbally running through the day and establishing our rules and boundaries. We set up consequences for not listening etc. Then, when a problem arises, all we have to do is follow the consequences that were set up in advance.

A dad always had a problem with his kids misbehaving in restaurants. To solve the problem, he took time to set consequences before leaving the house. He flatly stated that if the kids misbehaved in the restaurant, the entire family would get up and leave. Of course, nobody took this new rule very seriously, and they all agreed to the consequence. After a pleasant drive to the restaurant, everyone entered and was seated. All seemed to be going very well since the focus was on eating. It was a very hungry crew. They ordered food and drinks, and, as you might guess, it wasn't long before one kid started to misbehave. Dad very calmly called the waiter and paid the check. At that moment, the food came to the table. There were platters of tasty looking French fries and steaks. Dad stood up, looked at his kids, and said, "Let's go!" The kids couldn't believe he would actually leave all that food untouched. They left, and as you can imagine, future restaurant outings for that family were always more pleasant events.

8.5 SAFETY FIRST

Safety is one of my highest priorities, and I have missed airplane trips over this rule. If the team is not willing to keep each other safe, for whatever reason, we stay put and don't move until everybody can stay safe. This rule has really proven itself over the years, and I will not compromise on it. If one kid falls or gets hurt, I call a team meeting. Then, the kid who got hurt sits in 'timeout' since the child was not paying attention. It doesn't pay in my house to be sick or get hurt! It should never establish itself as an attention grabber.

I learned this rule from personal experience. As a child, I was frequently sick, and, therefore, received special treatment, special books, and special food. It was neat to get that extra attention. So, out of the blue, I developed strange high fevers. These sick episodes were so bad I was put in the hospital. Later, I realized that I had used my illness to get the attention I wanted.

9

Build a Team

Team Meetings

Team meetings are a great and vital tool for building teams. Yet, keep in mind that working as a team is not an easy task. It takes training to bring out the best in each team member, and it takes appreciation from each team member toward one another. A family is a great training ground for life, and team playing has to happen in every family, regardless of how small the family unit may be.

Team meetings in our household are a great tool for getting back on track when things get out of hand or when I personally get emotionally engaged.

For the team meeting, everybody begins with specifically one thing that personally worked and one thing that did not work. During the meeting, everyone applauds for both statements. No time must be spent agreeing or disagreeing with what worked or didn't work for another person or what should have been done. It's a time where every person has a turn at expressing what he or she thought worked and didn't work and nothing more.

After everyone has taken a turn, you can move to a family meeting if some solutions are needed. More than likely you will be able to look from a more detached (disengaged/neutral) position while in the family meeting and, therefore, make better decisions. You will notice that after each team meeting, your team will be much more united and connected. It will then be easier to accomplish individual and team goals. This method works because each person has had a chance to look at all issues and situations from an almost third party point of view. This stepping back, looking, and listening to others allows for objectivity to set in while emotions are put at bay.

The Objectives of Team Meetings:

1. To stop the world.

2. To clear the air; get things off everyone's mind.

3. To release emotions and tensions.

4. To build trust and team connection.

5. To build curiosity.

6. To build awareness by showing what is working and what is not working in the family. Enhances communication between family members.

When to Call a Team Meeting:

1. When safety is compromised.

2. When something is not working (rules are not being kept, or things are getting out of hand).

3. To acknowledge what's really working.

The Team Meeting Procedure:

1. The Adult "In-Charge" calls and runs a team meeting.

   • Anyone can go to the adult "In-Charge" and request a team meeting.

   • The adult who calls the meeting runs the team meeting.

2. The adult "In-Charge "asks, "What worked? What didn't work?"

3. Everyone has a turn saying one thing that worked and one thing that didn't work.

   • This incident report must be something personal.

   • This incident must be specific.

   • Don't let any member go into a story to try to explain why something did or did not work. Force all to be focused and specific.

4. If still necessary, address any other issues in a family meeting.

   • Say, "This isn't working; what do we do about it?" Create consequences, etc.

Team Meeting Rules:

1. Once a team meeting has been called, everyone drops everything and gathers together.

   • Everyone looks out for other team members.

   • Everyone makes sure that every member knows a team meeting has been called.

2. There is no order as to who goes first or whether it's "what worked" or "what didn't work" that is said first.

• The person running the meeting goes last.

3. Go through the process quickly.

   • If one person takes too long, go to the next one and come back to that person later.

   • If no person in the group volunteers to participate, you point to the next person.

4. No suggestions allowed from anyone. Each person must decide personally what did/didn't work.

5. No verbal agreements. Don't allow such comments as, "Yeah, that really didn't work," from anyone.

Example:

   • Naomi and Ian are arguing in the kitchen.

   • Micah comes to me and says, "We need a team meeting."

   • I (grown up "In-Charge") call a team meeting.

   • Everyone sits in the living room.

   • I ask, "What worked. What didn't work? Who wants to go first?" (In my family everyone wants to be first, so they all raise their hands.)

   • I pick Micah and ask, "What worked? What didn't work?"

   • Micah answers, " What worked was doing a back-flip on the trampoline and standing up!"

   • EVERYONE APPLAUDS!

   • "What didn't work was having an attitude about my math problem #16 today!"

   • EVERYONE APPLAUDS!

- Next, I pick Naomi and ask her, "What worked and what didn't work, Naomi?"

- She says, "What worked is showing Amy how to draw Pikachu."

- EVERYONE APPLAUDS

- What didn't work is arguing with Ian.

- EVERYONE APPLAUDS

This continues until everyone has been acknowledged. Most of the time the meeting then ends. If there is a need, we move to a family meeting. There I say, "So, what is the consequence for arguing— Ian and Naomi? You know you have to let the other person be right for everything they say during the next hour. If you can't do it, you get to do a cleaning assignment together and then let the other person be right for everything they say for one hour. (These are our personal consequences for arguing; you may pick something else.)

Acknowledgement Meetings

An acknowledgement meeting is yet another kind of meeting that we hold in our household, and I would advise you to do the same. The purpose of the acknowledgment meeting is to appreciate the individual team members.

Each person (including parents) gets in front of the group and is acknowledged for one thing that they did that really worked. They then take a bow or a curtsy or both while everyone applauds. Even though it is kind of embarrassing at first, it really feels good when you receive this praise. This meeting doesn't take long, and it has an amazing effect. Everyone feels important when united as a team, and the family becomes closer knit. Closely knit teams help contribute to everyone's happiness.

Families often fail to realize that most of their interactions may be negative when dealing with other family members. "American Mothers" reports that the opposite may be closer to the truth. Researchers, working out of Florida State, did a study on the American family. They placed observers in 7000 American homes to evaluate the mix between positive and negative interactions between family members in the 4 p.m. to 8 p.m. time period.

Before the study, the families estimated that 50% of their interactions would be positive, that is warm, kind and supportive and 50% negative, that is critical, demanding, and punishing. However, the facts showed that 80% of interactions were negative.

STEP-BY-STEP IMPLEMENTATION PLAN FOR RULE #1 - MOM HAS FUN!

Step 1 Start Right Away	Rationale
1) Call a family meeting and say: • "Here's what I experienced reading the book *Parenting Rule #1: Mom has Fun*" • "Here's what I would like to do in this family." 2) "Changes come from action. We're going to start slowly and see what works." 3) "We're going to start with simple steps: • Only one adult "In-Charge" at all times • Calling team meetings 4) Get curious with family members. What could make this family more efficient?	Rationale 1) Take advantage of the momentum and curiosity you have encountered while reading this book.
Institute Team Meetings	Rationale
1) Institute team meetings • Go over the rules for team meetings. Conduct a team meeting on the spot. 2) Continue to have team meetings whenever: • Safety is at stake • The 'space' is not clear • Something is not working • There is a shift in the energy (someone is having an attitude, etc)	Rationale 1) Stops the world. 2) Clears the air - deals with emotionally-charged situations that arise. 3) Equally acknowledges "what worked" and "what didn't work." (It's Okay to make mistakes) Keeps your team clear as to what works and doesn't work. 4) Keeps your team clear as to what works and doesn't work.

Then		Rationale
	1) Stay objective. Be curious. 2) Notice what's happening and be aware of the games being played. • WHY is not important— WHAT is happening is important. 3) Be aware of your emotions; observe your reactions 4) Notice what's working for you and what's not working for you; notice when you are having fun, and what's not fun 5) Provide feedback immediately without emotion • You did this; that's working, • You did this; that's not working	1) Awareness is the first step toward lasting change. 2) Instead of identifying with the emotion, try to focus on clear differences between what is working and what is not working and the impact it has had on you. Notice even the smallest of differences.

| Step 2 Establish Your Space | 1) Take a few days to look at what is *not* working for you in your family. Be objective and notice what's happening. WHY is *not* important; just note WHAT is happening. Notice when you get emotionally engaged.
2) Come up with rules to address those things (Table 2).
 • Have one or two rules in each category for each child.
 • Have appropriate consequences ready in case a child can't think of any.
3) Have a meeting to get a consensus with the adults in the house; modify the rules as needed.
4) Have a meeting with the entire family, and tell them the rules, and then have the children choose consequences for not following each rule.
 • For the same rule, every kid can have different consequences
 • If they can't think of a consequence, tell them what you would choose.
5) Types of Consequences :
 • Safety
 • Natural
 • Agreed upon in advance - logical
 • Consequences decided on the spot | **Rationale**
1) This is your space; you make the rules.
2) The rules have to work for you and your spouse.
 • Dad has fun
 • Mom has fun
3) Establishing the rules for your space builds safety and self-esteem in your children. |

Special Situations	1) Set rules before leaving.
• Restaurants	2) Communicate clearly *before* getting into a situation
• Airports	where you must enforce them.
• Vacation	
• Others	

In General	1) The games kids play will test you.	**Rationale**
	• Keep your word.	1. Builds Trust
	• Be consistent.	
	• Hold them accountable 100% of the time.	
	2) Respond *without* emotion	
	Don't decide for them.	
	Be happy with what they pick!	
	It may just be the consequence that works best.	

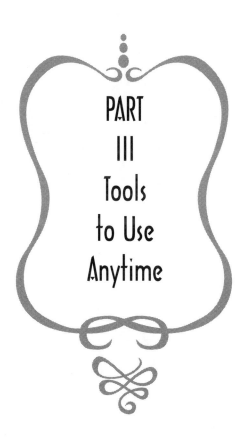

PART
III
Tools
to Use
Anytime

Tools to Use Anytime

Quick Reference Guide

Acknowledgement Works Better Than Discipline

A very important tool that all too often may be forgotten is that acknowledgement is the most effective form of discipline. Make sure you acknowledge things that are working the minute you notice them.

For example, we always include our children in what we call cleaning blitzes. These are organized cleaning tasks with one person in charge and a whole team to work. Everyone is part of the team regardless of age. Even our youngest, Amy, has been "assisting" like this ever since she could walk. When she was younger, we assigned tasks that were appropriate for her age, and we always made sure we acknowledged her when she did a good job. Amy is now five years old. Just the other day she cleaned the table and kitchen after lunch all by herself, since her brothers, sisters, and I had to go somewhere. Not only did she do a great job, but she also did it happily and was very proud of herself.

Get Their Attention— Speak with Intention.

Whenever speaking to your child, get the child's attention. Get on the child's level. Physically look the child straight in the eyes. And, then speak.

Do not speak at them. If you don't have the child's full attention, don't talk. Once you have gained that attention, speak with intention. Really mean what you say. A child intuitively feels when you mean what you are saying and can tell when you really don't. According to that feeling, the child will decide if listening is necessary or not. Intention is a powerful tool that can move even the greatest of obstacles. It also relaxes the child's system. If a child knows your intention and knows you are going to do whatever it takes to follow-through, the child most likely will step in line and assist you in getting what you want. If your intention is not clear, the child will probably test you first.

Build Trust with Your Child - NEVER Break Your Word

This rule is one of the most important. You must always keep your word so your children can build trust in you. This trust provides a level of security, putting body and mind at ease while increasing the child's self-worth.

If you can't hold a commitment, don't make it! If you can't enforce the rule, don't create it. It is better to have a few rules and never waiver than to have one hundred and fail to firmly enforce them.

> *Since I always followed through with my word, I had quite a bit of trust built up with my kids. Then, one night while going to the movies, one child started misbehaving. The consequence agreed-upon-in-advance— to turn the car around and go back home. But this time, I wanted to see the movie, so I thought it would be okay to make an exception. I decided to give them another chance. I did, and the evening went downhill from there. After giving one another chance, I had to give all five of them another chance, and on it went. It took me three months to undo that one night! I had broken my word and lost their trust. They had to test me, and test me, over and over again just to see if this time I really meant what I was saying!*

> GIVE ME
> RESPONSIBILITY,
> PLEASE!

Give Your Child Responsibility

Trusting your children is an effective way to build your relationship with them while helping them build personal self-esteem. If children are trustworthy, they can handle responsibility. In our house, we call it " being in charge of . . . "! This technique is a great way to give the child a bit of power.

Don't overdo it though. Only trust them for what they can be trusted to do. Here are a few simple rules: Always make sure your children feel and stay safe. Make sure they have trust before you assign any kind of responsibility. Make sure the duties you assign are age-appropriate. Responsibility should increase with age, not decrease.

Start assigning responsibility at an early age. A three-year old can have a limited amount of responsibility or duties. Even at this young age, children can pick up after themselves, put a dirty plate and cup in the sink, or let Mom know when the dog is out of food.

The child can also be responsible for certain cleaning assignments such as helping you or another adult or older child clean silver pieces or other duties. Give them duties that can be easily handled and ones that allow them a sense of pride when the job is finished.

Give Your Child Two Choices That You Can Live With

Another tool for building self-esteem is to give kids a choice between two alternatives. This works great with any age child. Just make sure you can live with both alternatives.

> *Keep these choices simple. For example, you might ask, "Do you want to wear the red or the green pajamas?" Your two-year old can make this choice. It will give the child a sense of power, and you really have nothing to lose by doing it. Or, you might say, "You can wipe the table or go to bed." These choices need to be neutral and cannot be a threat! Don't say, "You will either clean the table or go straight to bed." In this last statement, the word "will" changes the entire context. The wording makes the child feel as if the only right choice is to clean the table and that going to bed is punishment for making a wrong decision. Choices allow children to feel as if they have some control over their lives, and choices teach responsibility.*

I SAID NO, AND YOU CAN'T MAKE ME

Deal with Moods and Attitudes Immediately

Moods set in when kids focus their attention on themselves. They may think: I am right and everybody else is wrong, and I will prove it.

When in this negative mood, children often feel the world is against them.

What a lonely existence for a child to experience. As a loving parent, you can help your children snap out of negative thinking patterns by shifting their attention to something else. One of the best ways to do this is to give them an assisting assignment, particularly a cleaning assignment. These chores will take the child's attention away from self and put its focus on something else.

Assisting

People (including kids) are more effective human beings when their attention is not on themselves.

One way to remove attention from self is to focus on a task, which in turn keeps your mind busy. In my house, we call this assisting. When kids are assisting, they take on a task they can either do by themselves or can help an adult do. Simply by staying busy, the child's attention is taken off of personal thoughts and feelings and focused on the task at hand.

Cleaning Assignments

Cleaning chores are a great way to get kids back on track when a negative or low mood or attitude sneaks in. I see so many kids these days who are controlled by negative moods. These children are miserable, and it is so easy to pull them from the mood. It is never wise to leave them in a negative mood if the mood can be easily changed. Cleaning chores are simple tasks, yet they are useful and provide a child with a worthy way of lifting inner spirits. It is difficult to stay in a negative mood when one is busy since mental energy is focused on something other than self.

When a child first starts showing a negative attitude, first acknowledge it, and then provide feedback to help the child understand how emotions work. Hold the child accountable for letting negative feelings take control. In my house, we assign cleaning chores. The task isn't assigned for disciplinary reasons but rather to help the child move toward a more positive mental state.

> *Quite often, one of my kids will be given a cleaning assignment and angrily stomp into the bathroom. A few minutes later, I hear the child whistling. It is amazing how fast kids shift from a negative mood or attitude to a positive one.*

Give Your Kids a Way Out

When kids exhibit ill behavior or misbehave by displaying a mood or attitude, it is necessary to hold them accountable by providing them with appropriate feedback. If there is no awareness, the child may identify with or hold to a negative mood or inappropriate behavior. This could easily develop into a personal habit. The following games give them a way out.

When Awesome Bill starts to pout, he really becomes a different character. Start to call the pouting character "Pouting Paul" or some similar name. Most likely "Pouting Paul" will get a cleaning assignment. The moment "Pouting Paul" decides to snap out of his mood, he will be called Bill again.

Replace The Word "No"

Statistics show that by the time children reach two, they have heard the word "no" more often than any other word. For a lot of kids, "no" is actually the first word they say.

Using the word "no" invites a power struggle. Yes and no questions can be addressed in many other ways. "Maybe; we'll see; ask me after dinner; convince me that I should say yes." These statements eliminate a couple of hundred "nos". If the child's issue is really important, you will hear about it again later and can deal with it then.

The child asked, "Can I have a cookie?"
Mom says, "Ask me after dinner."
The child then says, "Can I sleep over at my friend's house?"
Mom's reply, " We will see."
The child asks, "Can I borrow your car?"
Dad says, "Convince me."

Reflective Listening

Reflective listening works well with older kids. You ask them a question and then let them talk. You don't answer with advice or solutions. You just stay curious and listen. When you understand the gist of what they said or recognize the emotion they experienced while talking, you reflect it back to them. They will hear what they just said from a new perspective and be able to formulate their own conclusions.

Mom: *"How was school today?"*

Mark: *"Oh, it really wasn't much fun!"*

Mom: *"So, it wasn't much fun."*
(Don't pressure for more. Be patient and wait.)

Mark: *"Yeah, my math teacher was really mean!"*

Mom: *"You seem to be upset because your math teacher was mean."*

Mark: *"Yes, and what she did was really not right. She told me to be quiet, and all I did was help Susan who always has a hard time. The teacher never takes time to explain it long enough for Susan, and then she yelled at me! It's really not fair."*

Mom: *"So, you got mad at your teacher for yelling at you."*

Mark: *"Yes, she got mad at me, and all I was doing was helping. She shouldn't do that! Helping people is a good thing!"*

Mom: *"I see what you are saying."*

Mark: *"If she ever does that again, I'll just leave the classroom!"*

Mom: *"You're still angry with her."*

Mark: *"You know, Mom, actually I like my math teacher very much, and I wonder if I went to her after class and just talked to her, and told her about Susan, and going slower, if that would help."*

Mom: *"That sounds like a very good solution, and it may work!"*

In this story, Mom uses reflective listening. She encourages her son to talk his way through the problem. Mark got the emotion off his chest and started to see solutions.

Have Them Find Solutions

Since it is no fun for me to come up with solutions for everyone's problems, I have a rule in my house. "Come to Mom with solutions." The consequence of coming to me with a problem is that I get to pick the solution, and they most likely won't like it. This rule eliminates about nine out of ten requests for solutions.

The Arguing Tree

One of my sons likes to argue about everything. Tamara, his teacher, invented the arguing tree in his honor. It's a big tall tree in the back yard that will listen to his arguing all day long! When he wants to argue, he can talk to the tree as long as he likes. The tree will "listen" or stay in place while he talks. That way he has a place to vent his emotions without the entire family listening to his arguing.

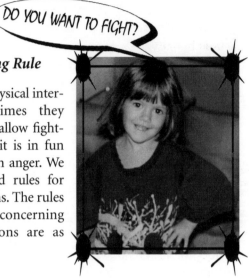

The Fighting Rule

Kids need physical inter-action. Sometimes they love to fight. I allow fight-ing as long as it is in fun and not done in anger. We have established rules for such interactions. The rules in my house concerning these interactions are as follows:

• First, you have to go to the adult in charge.

• You must ask for permission to fight.

• You have to make sure that you protect the other person at all times.

• Only the kids who asked permission may fight.

• Those fighting have a designated area.
  (In my house it is the trampoline).

• Finally, no one who agreed to fight can come to me later and whine.

If any of these rules are broken, I apply the consequence agreed up on in advance.

Welcome Mistakes

In our society, we learn very quickly that it is not okay to make mistakes. We learn that mistakes are bad, that they are wrong, and that making a mistake means failing. This is a great misconception! Many great inventions have only been possible because somebody was willing to make mistake after mistake. It took Edison 1000 tries before he invented the light bulb. When approached by a friend about his "failures" he answered: " I am not failing. I am finding out what doesn't work and eliminating possibilities." Successful people have one thing in common - they are willing to make mistakes.

We should not make children feel as if they are wrong when they make mistakes. Instead of focusing on doing things "right" and doing things "wrong," we need to focus on "what worked" and "what didn't work". In our team meetings, we don't acknowledge "what's right" and "what's wrong." We acknowledge "what worked" for that particular individual and "what didn't work." We then applaud both equally. We are acknowledging that making a mistake (doing something that didn't work) is as important as doing something that did work. There is no judgment about what someone did. Each person is his or her own judge. This creates a huge space of freedom where kids can "screw up" while it builds self-esteem and encourages your kids to take risks and learn from mistakes.

So welcome the spirit of curiosity in your child that makes him or her willing to make mistakes!

Do It as If Your Life Depends on It

In my house we have a rule: Do it as if your life depends on it! Putting all of your energy into a task creates a certain intensity, and it is also a game. Just imagine how well you could do a job if your life depended on it?

It really makes the kids perform at their best, while working and playing. Throwing your entire energy into a task also excludes space for thinking negative thoughts or having a bad attitude. When in the "do it as if" mode, you have to get very creative, have your attention focused outward, and perform at your best. I profoundly feel life should be played in this manner. A person's vitality and satisfaction in life truly does depend on it. Give your task at hand your best regardless of what else is going on in life, and you will see that life will become much more enjoyable.

Physically Practice the Behavior That Works or Doesn't Work

Practicing positive behavior is such a neat and easy tool to help adjust inappropriate behavior. All you do is role-play the behavior you want to instill in the child and continue with the exercise until your child has the skill perfected. Take turns when role-playing. Make it a game and see who can do it better. Your child will love the time spent interacting with you and will proudly apply the new learned behavior on stage.

> *If your child is interrupting you inappropriately, try this exercise. Teach your child how to properly interrupt you. First, you state that there is an appropriate way to interrupt, stating that to get your attention, the child should gently tap you once on the shoulder. Ask your child to wait patiently while you pretend to talk to someone else. Then, stop and really give the child your full attention and ask what he or she would like. Role-play this behavior until your child feels comfortable with it, and it becomes natural behavior. Then, use it on stage.*

Identify Who Has the Problem. Let That Person Find a Solution

None of us like for others to solve our problems, and our kids are no different. Yet, we grown-ups always think we know what is best. We think we know the right way to handle problems because we are older and, surely, wiser, but let us look at this logic. When someone tells you what to do or how to solve your problem, there is a good chance your first reaction would be to go against what the person advised, and do it your way. I know I have reacted that way at times, and I've observed the same reaction in hundreds of kids.

To avoid making my children feel inadequate in the problem-solving arena, and to let the solution be their solution, I really push my kids to find their own solutions. I may assist them by reflective listening or one of the other tools, but I've learned that if they discover a solution, even if it's not as good as mine, they are much more likely to use that solution to work through the problem.

Stimulate All Intelligences Every Day

Howard Gardner has developed a theory that states different people have 8 1/2 different potential intelligences. The development of these intelligences can greatly affect one's learning style.

In his book *Intelligence Reframed*, Gardner defines intelligence as follows:

Intelligence is a biopsychological potential that is ours by virtue of our species membership. That potential can be realized to a greater or lesser extent as a consequence of the experiential, cultural and motivational factors that affect a person.

When I discovered his theory, I was fascinated. Gardner points out how important it is not only to stimulate each one of the intelligences but also to have material presented in your "strong intelligence" in order for you to best retain that information. Each day, give children activities that access each one of the eight intelligences and then notice which ones are stronger in each child. If they are struggling with a concept, explain it to them using their "strong" intelligence, and then observe them as the weak ones develop.

The 8 1/2 Intelligences from the book *Intelligence Reframed* by Howard Gardner:

1. LINGUISTIC: involves sensitivity to spoken and written language, the ability to learn languages, the capacity to use language to accomplish a certain goal.

2. LOGICAL-MATHEMATICAL: involves the capacity to analyze problems logically, carry out mathematical operations and investigate issues scientifically.

3. MUSICAL: entails skills in performance, composition and appreciation of musical patterns.

4. BODILY-KINESTHETIC: entails the potential of using the whole body or parts of the body (like the hand or the mouth) to solve problems or fashion products.

5. SPATIAL: the potential to recognize and manipulate the patterns of wide space (navigators, pilots) as well as the patterns of more confined areas (sculptors, architects, surgeons).

6. INTERPERSONAL: A person's capacity to understand the intentions, motivations, and desires of other people and, consequently, to work effectively with others. (Salesperson, leaders, actors, teachers).

7. INTRAPERSONAL: The capacity to understand oneself, to have an effective working model of oneself - including one's own desires, fears and capacities - and to use such information effectively in regulating one's own life.

8. NATURALISTIC: The capacity to recognize and classify numerous species- flora and fauna- of one's environment.

9. The candidate ninth intelligence is called existential intelligence—the intelligence that asks big questions. Gardner is continuing to accrue evidence relevant to existential intelligence.

Howard Gardner 8 Intelligences

Interpersonal	Persuasive speeches, performing, speaking in meetings, team-activities
Intrapersonal	Journals, art
Musical/Rhythmic	Have music always playing, do singing with motion, memorize songs with motion o Classical - Baroque o Folk o Musicals o Performing
Logical/Mathematical	Sequencing, math problems, patterns Acknowledging when they make patterns in a beaded necklace, for example
Spatial/Visual	Making doll clothes from a pattern they create. Building.
Verbal/Linguistic	Writing and sharing journals Reading 2nd language daily
Body/Kinesthetic	Singing songs with motion, building, sewing, spelling with shape letters, stringing, clapping and bowing in meetings
Naturalistic	Planting flowers, watching birds, learn about nature on walks

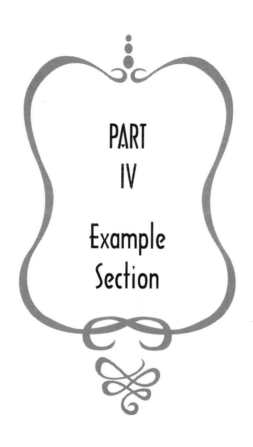

PART
IV

Example
Section

Games of
Manipulation Kids Play
and Possible Solutions

11

Games Children Play

Earlier we discussed the "games" kids play. Children aren't wrong for playing these games. They use them to learn about the world of emotions just as we did. But, never forget that they love the feeling of power they get from emotionally manipulating adults to get what they think they want.

Our goal as parents is to hold them accountable so that they can learn to *control* their emotions rather than being *controlled* by them. In other words, they need to learn to have emotions by choice rather than being run by them. To do that, we must first be aware of the games our kids are playing. Once we understand those games, we hold them accountable by giving them feedback and/or consequences.

Quick Reference Guide

Our focus in this section will include examples of different games children will play and possible solutions. Remember this simple rule of thumb: If your child is not sharing his or her brilliance, the child is most likely caught in an emotional state. The most important service you can do for your child is to help the child snap out of any negative emotional state! It takes curiosity and understanding on your part to do this.

Hurting Others

Hurting others with physically aggressive actions, including choking, biting, hair pulling, hitting, kicking, pinching, pushing, scratching, slapping, and spitting is violence. Violence is a learned response that gives a child what he or she wants in the short term. Humans have used the tactic of overpowering an opponent to take from others since before history was even documented. Our goal is to teach a child to get what is desired without damaging another person. This concept is an art form in and of itself.

Solution: The first step is to determine if the game is really hurtful. A very small child may not be aware that pulling your hair hurts or biting you hurts. In that case, it is important to show them by example that pulling your hair or biting actually hurts. Remember to do this when you are not emotionally engaged. Make sure that you are merely showing them how it feels and NOT doing it as payback or punishment. Then, teach them a behavior that works. Take their hand and gently move it over your hair, and say: "Here. That is what I really like. That feels great. Do it like this!"

With older children who know what they are doing, it works best if you have agreed on a consequence in advance. When they hurt someone, hold them accountable by enforcing the consequences. If the situation repeats itself over and over, it's time to look at it a little more closely. Role-play the situation with the child to understand how he or she is feeling, and then role-play a behavior that works.

Disrespect

> **Example 1:** *A three and one half year old child yells,* "*Mommy, I hate you.*"
>
> **Example 2:** *As Mom pulled into the driveway to pick up a notebook, her first-grade daughter was waiting in the car. They exchanged a few sentences when all of a sudden a very disrespectful,* "*Can't we just go now?*" *came from the child in the car.*

A child's aggressive, unruly behavior can result from confusion over an adult's behavior. Sometimes the adult is not being respectful and is merely trying to dominate a smaller human being. Domination incites fear and is often followed by punishment. When you dominate your children, you make them feel as if they have done something wrong, and they generally associate wrong actions with punishment. You are using fear to get what you want rather than agreeing on the consequence for actions and implementing those consequences. Making children accountable for actions teaches responsibility. Punishment creates ill feelings. When an adult dominates a child, neither party respects the other. A bright human being is naturally willing to please, learn, share and co-operate. The most effective way to build human potential is mutual respect, appreciation, and immediate feedback.

You and your child have a partnership relationship that requires attention and communication. Holding the child accountable in an atmosphere of clear non-judgmental communication and mutual respect enables the child to overcome impulsiveness and consciously develop self-discipline. The child will learn to act as a well-mannered, respectful human being and is trained into self-disciple and away from impulsiveness.

Solution: Make sure that your intention is respectful and that you are not just trying to dominate the child. Then, clearly communicate what you expect from the child. Very often, simply giving feedback will be enough to handle a communication of that sort. For example, you may say something like this: "Your tone of voice was very disrespectful. Try again!"

Disappearing

Disappearing is a *dangerous* way to get attention.

One bright young fellow called Aaron found disappearing to be a very exciting way to get attention. Once when Aaron's parents took him to a big museum, he left the family group and disappeared. He immediately went to the nearest security guard and reported himself lost. The guard took him to the information desk, and the attendant announced over the loud speaker so everyone in the museum could hear: "Would the parents of Aaron MacKay please come to the information booth." His parents rushed over, relieved that their son was Okay. Aaron had been in the attention-getting arena for at least twenty minutes.

It turned out that Aaron had already disappeared four other times that year. He always went to the nearest security guard, and they would announce his name over the PA system. His mom started to see the game.

Solution: Mom and Aaron sat down and looked at what had happened. Without making Aaron feel that he did anything wrong, Mom acknowledged the disappearing game and pointed out the danger of playing the game. Aaron knew he was caught, and since Mom didn't blame him for doing something wrong, he could easily admit it. Then, they looked at different ways Aaron could get attention. Finally, they picked a very strong consequence for Aaron. If he disappeared again in a public place, he would lose one week of baseball. It worked. Aaron has stopped disappearing in public places. This tactic worked because Aaron knew he would pay a price if he disappeared in public again, and yet, he was able to openly admit what he had been doing and was given a chance to correct the situation without being punished for it.

Getting Dressed - Dawdling

Slow and picky, little Magi is in control. It is 7:00 a.m. and four-year old Magi needs to be in preschool by 8:00. Magi's mother needs to be at work by 8:30 a.m. There is no time to waste! But, every morning it's the same story. A mother-daughter battle ensures. First, Magi won't get out of bed. Her mother has to go to her room ten times to ask her daughter to get up. Then, after she finally gets up, Magi whines, "Mom, I can't put my socks on! Mom, I need help."

Kathy's mother looks at her watch. It's 7:30. Stressed and aggravated, her mother helps Magi with her socks and yells, "Hurry up. You need to eat. We need to leave!" Kathy's mom is now emotionally engaged. When it is least needed, Kathy whines, "Mom, I don't want to wear that dress—no, not that one. It itches! I am not going to wear this." By the time they leave, Kathy's mother is mad.

This is a very common problem. It's a scenario I hear at almost every Responsive Parenting Seminar I hold. What a way to start your day! Every day!

Kids are very smart. They know that the best time to push your buttons is when there is little time and the lack of time will make you feel pressured.

Solution: Here are three different ways of dealing with this situation:

1. Make getting up and getting dressed into a game. Race each other or race the clock. "Whoever's ready first wins!" Or, "Whoever's ready by 8:00 a.m. wins!"
   Making it a game works especially well with little ones.

2. Have the kids decide the night before what clothes will be worn. Give them two choices you can live with, and let them choose.

3. Set up a consequence in advance. A good one is that the child has to get up earlier, which, of course, means going to bed sooner.

4. You also could use the three solutions in combination.

Getting Dressed – "Badly"

Little Kathy is a very pretty girl who just turned four and is ready to conquer the world, yet there is one problem. She insists on dressing herself, and she also insists on doing her own hair. Now, this might not be a problem for an older child, but a four year old can make a few flaws in judgment. Her mother, who until six months ago had no problem dressing Kathy or fixing her daughter's hair, now does not know what to do. Not only does Kathy fix her hair, but she fixes it very badly, and to compound the problem, she dresses herself in mismatched outfits. Stubbornly, the child refuses any assistance from her mother. If her mother persists in helping, Kathy throws a big tantrum. Obviously, this situation leads to a big power-struggle before Kathy and her mother leave the house.

Kathy's mother finally gives up and takes her daughter to the daycare, dressed in her mismatched outfits. Kathy mother is bothered by her daughter's looks. As conqueror, Kathy proudly walks out of the battle the winner, a win that gives more power to the child's game.

Situation: Since Kathy's mother is so attached to the way Kathy presents herself, it is an open invitation for Kathy to use it as a measurement of power. Although this is the age where children want to be more independent and in charge, if done without engaging in a power struggle, children still can be easily redirected. Remember *Rule # 1: Mom Has Fun.*

Solution: Kathy and her mother have a meeting. Kathy's mother provides feedback to her daughter by exposing the button pushing game and acknowledges how she, the parent, let herself get emotionally engaged. She wants to know if her daughter sees the game. With a big smile on her face, Kathy replies, "Yes." Her mother then says, "Remember the new rule in the house? Mom has fun! Well, how can you make sure this is fun for me?"

The first solution they devise is that each of them will take turns deciding what Kathy wears and how she fixes her hair. One day Kathy can decide. The next her mother gets to decide. Kathy's mother wasn't happy with that solution, so she suggests that as the mom, she gets her turn before school and Kathy gets her turn before going out to play with friends.

They also start a fashion show game to be played as a reward for every week that there is no struggle over dressing. During this time, Kathy presents a fashion show to her mother, and if her mom is up to it, she can participate. Kathy gets to pick her mother's dresses and fixes her mother's hair. If the rules are broken, Kathy, as a consequence, does not go to her friends and, of course, they would not play the fashion show game. This solution works well for them.

Eating Habits

Trying New Food: Many a parent wonders just how one teaches a child to love anything that is good and healthy. Ironically, it seems that most foods that are good for us are the very ones we must acquire a taste for before we learn to enjoy them. For example, I believe that brown rice is good for my children, so I decided to teach my children to like brown rice.

Solution: At our house, if you don't like a particular food, you don't have to eat it. However, if you choose to not eat what is served, you will not get anything else until the next meal. No snacks and no whining about being hungry are allowed. This basic rule takes a lot of the pressure out of making kids eat what is cooked.

When I started serving brown rice, the kids wouldn't eat it. So, for weeks we had brown rice, and the kids couldn't snack between meals. Finally, they broke down and decided to try it. Now, they like the taste, and they're open to trying almost any new food.

Mom...Mom...Mom...Mom...Mom...

Does Not Like It— Not One Little Bit: My son Micah refuses to eat canned tuna. Otherwise, he is a happy, healthy eater. He enjoys fresh fruits and vegetables, including raw carrots, and eats most everything his family eats.

Situation: Since Micah is a very good eater, in general, and not picky with anything else, we allowed him to avoid eating tuna. As long as it doesn't become a game of manipulation, it is perfectly okay with me for a child to dislike a few foods.

Picky eater: Brian was five years old when his mother brought him to visit. He would only eat French fries, noodles, and sweets. When I talked to his mom about it, she said, "Oh, he is a very picky eater, but so am I. Any other kind of food he just plays with." As a curious mother, she wanted to know what else she could do about Brian's picky eating habits.

Solution: I told her to set new boundaries. Say something like, "You have to eat what is served, or you will not get anything else until the next meal." Start with a mixture of food that includes one of his favorites. If he eats what's served, really praise him. Most likely he will test the rules and only eat the foods he likes, so he'll go hungry for a couple of days. Stick to your rules and only serve food at the table. No snacks! As long as it's his choice, once he gets hungry enough, he'll try some of the healthier foods. Then, slowly start to change the menu to a healthier choice.

Note: This approach only works if everyone else in the child's environment is playing the same game.

Making Excuses

Making excuses is a way to say, "Yes, but..." And, usually it is blaming someone else.

> *"My paper was late because I left it in my friend's car,*
> *and he lost his key."*
> *"I didn't do my homework because Billy wasn't home,*
> *and I didn't have the assignment."*
> *"I couldn't hear the teacher."*
> *"Alice ate my cake, so I had to take her eraser."*

The list of excuses goes on. When a child understands accountability for personal actions, there are no excuses.

Solution: Notice the game. Point out that in this scenario, someone else is wrong and is, therefore, to blame. If someone else is wrong, that person must be punished.

One possible consequence is to have the child write down ten different excuses that could have been used instead for the same situation. Or, have the child write ten things that is likeable about the person who was blamed for the inappropriate actions.

Ignoring: Greg is eight years old and practices selective hearing very well. If his mom wants him to do something, she has to repeat it ten times before he responds. Of course, if it's something he wants to do, he responds right away.

Solution: Mom and Greg sit down, and mom points out the game. (Of course, Greg was already aware of the game.) Together they pick a consequence for ignoring. Greg loves electronic games, so they decide that ignoring means he loses his game time for a day.

Like many kids, Greg tests the boundaries, so the first time his mother asks him to do something, he doesn't respond. Relying on her new tactics, she marches right over to him, takes his head in her hands, and tells him to look her in the eye. With his full attention, she says, "Greg, you're playing the ignoring game. You just lost a day of electronic games. Are you ready to follow instructions now?" Startled, Greg immediately jumps up and does what he is told.

Getting Injured

Little Mark, a seven-year old, knows exactly how to get her mom's attention; he gets injured, and it works, every time, guaranteed! Since his games work, Mark has developed this attention getting technique so well he has crafted it into an art. He gets hurt all the time, and the doctors in the emergency room all know his name.

Solution: After looking at the dynamics behind the "getting hurt" game, Mark's mother decides to try a new approach. She first talks with her son, telling him that people get hurt when they fail to pay attention to what they are doing. She explains that if he isn't paying attention, there should be a consequence for that action. She sets down a new consequence for not paying attention and getting hurt – a timeout. Then, whenever Mark gets hurt, his mother gives him timeout. Timeout temporarily stops the world. The child has to sit down with hands on knees. This is not punishment but is a time to recollect thoughts and actions. After the timeout, Mark's mom asks, "Are you ready to stay safe?"

The next, equally important, step is to find new ways for Mark to get his mother's attention. It just happens that Mark loves to act. He is very talented and very dramatic. His mother signs him up for a theater group where he receives lots of good attention for some very good drama. It works. Mark doesn't get injured anymore.

Getting Hurt at Bedtime: Rule #1 includes the priority of safety first. Cecilia, a two and a half year old is as bright as a light bulb. She has energy all day long, playing throughout the day, and she learns very quickly. When evening rolls around, she gets tired and hits her head and cries. Her parents drop everything and pay attention to Cecilia and start their "good night, sweet child" ritual. Except that by this time, Cecilia is so tired that she resists everything. It takes her mom and dad hours and lots of energy to get her to bed.

Solution: Cecilia's mother realizes that her daughter is literally crying for attention, habitual structure, and a reasonable way to start the bedtime process. Cecilia's mother tells her child that from now on every night when the clock reads 7:30, it means it is time for mom or dad to read Cecilia and her little brother Jake their bedtime stories. Cecilia brushes her teeth and puts on her pajamas beforehand so she is ready for story time right when the clock reaches 7:30. She knows that if she isn't ready by 7:30, there will be no bedtime story. This structure works well for the entire family. The best part is that Cecilia doesn't have to bang her head to let everyone know it is bedtime.

Getting Back out of Bed

Three-year old John is quite a little talker. He loves to keep everyone entertained, especially at bedtime. He usually goes to bed without a problem, but after his bedtime story, he finds a hundred excuses to sneak back out. "Mom, I need another hug." "Mom, I need a sip of water. I'm scared." Every night is torture for his mom and dad.

Solution: After role-playing the situation in Responsive Parenting, his mother realizes she is engaging in quite a power struggle every night. Little John ends up the big winner - proof of his power. To solve the problem, she sits him down and tells him they need to find another solution to make bedtime more fun for mom. They talk about him becoming the new "going to sleep" champion. On top of that, champions earn a second story the next night. Intrigued by becoming a "going to sleep champion, Johnny readily agrees. What really wins him over, though, is the promise of the second story. It is well worth going to sleep right away to earn that second story.

Interrupting

A true leader, four-year old Mara is very popular with all her friends. She is also very impatient when she wants something. Her mom has a home business and is on the phone. She sometimes locks herself into a room to get away from Mara's constant interruptions.

Solution: Mara is very smart and learns quickly, so her mom did a bit of role-playing with her, teaching her daughter how to interrupt in a way that works for mom. They pretend that mom is on the phone. Mara comes in, taps her mother on the shoulder once, and patiently waits until her mother is ready to address Mara's needs. By approaching Mom this way, there is a much greater likelihood that Mara will get what she wants.

Then, Mom sets down a consequence for interrupting. If Mara interrupts in a way that doesn't work for mom, she loses one day with her friends.

Playing Adults against Each Other

Johnny is very good at this game. He knows how to play his parents against each other. He knows who to ask and how to ask to get what he wants. He knows that mom has a rule that if you don't eat at lunch, you won't get anything until dinner. The minute dad gets home, Johnny asks him for a treat, and, of course, dad says, "Yes," not knowing what happened at lunch. The next minute Johnny is licking an ice cream right in front of his mom!

Solution: There is only one grown-up "In-Charge" at a time. If mom is "In charge," when dad comes home he can simple say, " I don't know, Johnny. I am not "In-Charge." Go ask the person "In-Charge."

If mom needs a break and wants dad to take over when he gets home, the first step is for dad to find out the status of things, and then take over the task of being In-Charge. Remember, whoever is "In-Charge" puts down the rules that apply for that time period. It's Okay for parents to have different rules as long as the kids know whose rules apply and when. However, it does help to have some general house rules that both parents use.

Pouting

Seven-year old Mary loves to get her way. One of her most effective tools is pouting. When things don't go her way, she sticks out her lower lip, hangs her head, and goes into one of her pouting moods. It drives her mom absolutely crazy and often, after hours of pouting, her mother will give in to relieve personal anxiety.

Solution: After a Responsive Parenting seminar, her mom could clearly see how Mary pushes her mother's buttons by pouting. Mary points this out to her daughter, and they pick a consequence for pouting. Since pouting can easily become a mood, they actually pick two consequences. They agree that pouting first results in a cleaning assignment. They then agree that if Mary doesn't do the cleaning assignment right away, the child forfeits a Pokemon card and gets a timeout until she is ready to do her cleaning assignment.

Temper Tantrums

As a young woman, I would see children throwing those nasty temper tantrums in the grocery store, and I would swear to myself (rather self-righteously) that my kids would never behave that way. A few years later, once I had my kids, I was amazed to find myself in various public places with my own offspring throwing dramatic temper tantrums. My compassion for other parents increased a thousand-fold with the first public tantrum. I also realized how little I had previously understood normal childhood development.

Some specialist suggests that if you ignore temper tantrums, they will go away.

One mom had this to say:

"The books I read while my second child was in her 'Terrible Twos' said to ignore temper tantrums and they would go away. I remember letting her lay on the floor in the restaurant and yell because she could not have candy. We pretended to ignore her. This advice has really cost my daughter. She is in her twenties and still has temper tantrums.

"Nobody won. She did not get what she wanted when she threw the temper tantrum, and I didn't get what I wanted. In pretending to ignore her, I also didn't teach her what I wanted."

Children throw temper tantrums:

• To win a power-struggle

• To get your attention

• When exposed to anger and going into overload (reflection)

Solution: The following approach works best if you're not emotionally engaged. If you don't let your children push your buttons, the temper tantrum will quickly end. This does not mean to ignore it. It just means dealing with it in the most effective way possible.

When a tantrum starts, don't try to stop it. Just make sure the child engaged in it is safe while working through it.

Sometimes it is best to sit with the child to stop head banging or similar actions that can injure the child. And, keep the child safe at all times. For example, if the child is in traffic, move to a safe area and then let the child work through the tantrum. After the tantrum is over, hold your child for a few minutes.

Once the child has calmed down, it's time to look at the consequence for the "temper tantrum" game. Unless this is the first time, you should already have some pre-determined consequences. (Remember, Rule #1: Mom Has Fun - make sure to pick consequences that work for you!)

One of the most effective consequences for public misbehavior is to give up the activity immediately and go home. Remember, no one ever said being a parent was convenient. Your job is to ruthlessly watch for games and enforce consequences. Holding young children completely accountable for inappropriate behavior is the most effective strategy in the long run. It will save you hours and days of frustration and maybe even months and years. Your efforts will pay off when you see your little ones grow into respectful adolescents and adults with happy attitudes and productive habits who know how to respond since you have enhanced their intelligence by enforcing nonjudgemental feedback and consequences.

Solutions for the Grocery Store Tantrum: Grocery store temper tantrums are easy to eliminate with some advance planning. In addition to reviewing the ground rules and the consequences for temper tantrums and other misbehavior, decide with your child ahead of time what can and can't be bought while shopping. At the store, continually acknowledge the behavior you want by praising it: "Johnny, you just walked by all that candy and didn't ask for one piece. I really like going to the store with you when you can enjoy helping me shop." Kids are very smart and are generally willing to learn whatever we are willing to teach them.

Self-pity or Poor Me Attitude

Self-pity is a strong root for the moods and attitudes that hinder our effectiveness. "I just can't do it!" "I try my best, and I still can't do it!" "You neglect me. You don't help me. You don't love me." "The other kids beat me up." boo hoo boo hoo How many parents have heard these tales of woe? Poor me, and it's someone else's fault! Going into a negative mood of self-pity does feel terrible and seems so real. We all know the feeling. The truth is only you can feel sorry for yourself if you have the attention on yourself.

Solution: The best service you can do when your children start to wallow in self-pity is to try to think of new and inventive ways to help them shift their attention. The first step is to provide feedback, and then if it is my child, I usually give them a cleaning assignment. Sometimes, the cleaning assignment can only be done after a timeout, since you can't force anyone to do anything. I might say, "You are full of self-pity right now. Sit down right here with your hands on your knees until you are ready to go and clean the bathroom." Since sitting in a timeout to solve the problem is boring, a child will do the chore, since it is the only way out of the timeout.

Sloppiness

It is easier to be around people who are considerate of the space you share and who know how to organize their possessions. I was recently talking to a woman whose business is helping other people get organized. I asked her what she considers to be the most useful skill she can teach her children. "Tidiness!" she replies without hesitation. No one likes to be around people who are sloppy and who wait for others to clean up after them. What do you want in your surroundings?

Sloppiness is learned. Tidiness is learned. Younger children love to clean and pay attention to details. In the Montessori program, adults give little kids silverware to clean, and the kids love it.

Train your children with tasks that they can really do well. They will learn to enjoy doing a good job. Smaller children may not be able to sweep the floor perfectly, but, with your guidance and assistance, they can learn to love doing these tasks. Older children should have more responsibility and more difficult assignments.

Tattle-telling

Sometimes it's appropriate for your child to let adults know what is going on with other children. Sometimes, however, the information is delivered simply to stir things up and to make sure that the "guilty" child gets in trouble with the authority figure. This is a clever way to get power.

The way to distinguish between accurate reports from the field and tattle-telling is to look at the motive. What is the child's motive in delivering the communication?

Solution: This is another opportunity to get curious. The first thing I usually do is identify who has the problem.

- If I don't have a problem with what's happening, my answer is, "This isn't my problem. It's yours. You need to find a solution."

- If I do have a problem with what's going on, I usually tell them to come up with a solution that works. They know that if they don't, I will solve it, and nobody will like my solution.

- If there are more than two kids involved in the disagreement, I usually give them a cleaning assignment as a team, if necessary after a timeout, so they can come together as a team again.

Time Pressure

At times we all have a need to go somewhere and arrive punctually. One of the perfect times to engage adults in power struggles is when they are under the gun. For example, if everyone needs to be ready by 6 p.m. to arrive somewhere on time, the adults are under pressure. Adults are very vulnerable under such circumstances.

Raul, a twelve year old, has to do everything on his own timetable. Whenever it is time to go some place, Raul starts to drag. He can't find his socks. Then his shoes are missing, etc. His mom and dad get completely frustrated and usually end up being late.

Solution: Again, the first step is to name the game. Raul admitted he enjoyed the power he felt in this situation. His parents and Raul decided to pick an extra-tough consequence so he would think twice before making everyone late again. Since he really liked hanging out with his friends, they agreed that for each minute he delayed the family, he would lose one hour with his friends. After that, Raul got retrained very quickly.

Pressuring an Adult

"Mom, you said I could get this Pokemon package. Let's go right now. I want it right now, Mom. Please! You told me I could!"

I call this putting pressure on adults.

Solution: Give them feedback first and then a consequence.

"You are putting pressure on me to get something you want right now. That doesn't work for me! When you put pressure on me, it makes me want to not give the Pokemon package to you at all. So, here is my solution. We will get you a Pokemon package, but we will do it when it works for me. Every time you put pressure on me to get it, we will postpone it by one day."

Whining

In the Store: Like most children, three year old Rose really looks forward to going grocery shopping with her mom. Her goal is to have her mom get her a treat to eat while they shop. Rose has developed a strategy that works. The child manipulates her mom into giving her a treat every time they go shopping.

When they first enter the store, Rose quickly finds a sweet and says, "Mom, I want that". Her mom is ready for this behavior and firmly states the rule: "We're not buying anything sweet today." Rose hears her mom, accepts the no answer, and moves down the aisle to the next temptation. When Rose spots the next sweet, she starts playing to win. A master whiner, Rose begins a high-pitched whine, "I want a treat, Mommy! Please buy me this candy. I'll be good if you just buy it for me."

This performance usually engages her mom who perceives her daughter's behavior as nasty. Rose's mom reacts out of anger and judgment. " Rose, nooooooo!" shouts angry Mom. That is when Rose knows that her mom is going to lose. Rose adds volume to her whine and begins to cry. With artfully executed timing, Rose starts her final power play and refuses to move from the spot. Other people start to watch the scene, and her mother's anger turns to embarrassment and shame. Rose has her mother trapped. Her mother really wants to get the attention off Rose, and she is a busy woman who needs to get the shopping finished. Mentally, Rose's mom thinks that she might as well give her daughter the candy in an effort to get the child to behave. What difference will giving in make anyway?

Solution: After the advanced parenting class, this mother sat Rose down and said, "You know, Rose, you're three years old now. It's time for you to have some more responsibility. Here's what we are going to do. We're going to start a system where you can get four sweets a month. You get to choose what you want to buy and when. I'll give you four stickers each month. When we go shopping, you take your stickers with you, and if you decide to buy a sweet under $1, you can trade me the sticker for the sweet. That will be the only way you can get something while we're shopping. If you pressure me and start whining, from now on, we'll leave the store immediately, and you'll have a time-out when we get outside."

Mother and daughter agreed. Rose was very proud of her stickers, and the first few times the plan worked very well. Then, one day Rose forgot her stickers, and she started her old pattern again. At the first whine, her mother took her daughter by the hand, left the store, and made Rose sit outside in timeout. After a couple of minutes, she reminded Rose of their agreement and asked Rose if she were ready to go back in and keep her word. Rose agreed. They passed the first sweet, and Rose was quiet. Now, it was mom's turn to really acknowledge her daughter for not whining. Rose was very proud of herself and from that day on, shopping with Rose was a much more pleasurable experience.

My Way

Bill is six years old, and he's a very sensitive little boy. He has high expectations of himself, and when things are not going his way he whines. Mom has tried everything. You name it, and she tried it: timeouts, cleaning assignments, sending him to his room, having him lose privileges, etc. Nothing seems to work.

Solution: After the Advanced Parenting seminar, his mom sat down with Bill and said, "You know Bill, every time things don't go the way you think they should, you start whining. I really don't know what we can do about this. We have to find a solution because that whining really gets on my nerves. You need to give me a solution that will work."

At first, Bill was not very cooperative. His answer was, "I don't know." So, his mom said, "If you don't come up with something that will work, I'll just have to try things that are really hard for you, such as one week with no Nintendo or one week no TV." This got Bill's curiosity, and he said, "Okay, I think I could do a headstand every time I whine." Well, that suggestion made his mom laugh, but she agreed to try it. It worked beautifully! Every time Bill whined, she would say, "You're whining. Go do a headstand." He would do a headstand, which made him laugh every time and got him into a completely different mood. ****Nicole, what if Bill whines BECAUSE he wants to do a headstand? Will he not whine more often?

Whiny Voice

Little Max is two years old. He is very smart and already talks really well. The only problem is that he starts to whine the minute he wants something.

"Mommy, can you help me here? Mommy, Sara is doing this to me."

Solution: This mom sat down with Max in a quiet moment and said, "Max, I want to do a voice game with you. I want to see in how many ways you can say, 'Sara took my red truck away from me!' I'll go first, and you tell me what kind of voice I'm using." His mom started with a whiny voice, then a stern voice, then an angry voice and then an awesome voice. Max loved guessing which voice was which and couldn't wait for his turn to say the phrase. When he got to the awesome voice, his mom said, "Wow, I really like this voice. That is my favorite voice of all." They played the game for a while longer, and each time his mom especially acknowledged the awesome voice and pointed out the whiny voice. When dad came home, mom had Max show his dad his whiny voice and his awesome voice, and, of course, dad liked the awesome voice much better, too. From then on, every time Max whined, his parents would say, "Max, say that again in your awesome voice." It worked quickly and changed Max's attitude in many situations.

Whining out of Frustration

Alexandria is eight years old. She is a very smart child and also very impatient. When she cannot accomplish something immediately, she gets frustrated and starts whining.

Solution: Every time Alexandria would go into this whiny mood her teacher would say, "Oh, look at this; it's Whiny Wanda. I wonder where Awesome Alexandria is? Whiny Wanda has to go sweep or sit outside until Awesome Alexandria comes back." This worked very well. Calling her Whiny Wanda when she was whining helped Alexandria to stay detached from her mood. It wasn't her whining. It was that Wanda girl. She was able to get over it more quickly. Using the two names also helped the teacher address the two completely opposite sides of Alexandria differently

Whining to Get Your Way

One mom was being driven up the wall by her five-year old daughter's very imaginative high-pitched whine.

Solution: After the Responsive Parenting seminar, this mom immediately had a team meeting. After the team meeting, she and her daughter talked about consequences for whining. The whiner extraordinaire, with great curiosity in her eyes, suggested that anytime mom or dad caught her at the whining game she would clean the bathrooms.

When I spoke with the child's mom a week later, she had started holding her daughter accountable. She was having her daughter clean the bathrooms every time she whined. The daughter was gladly cleaning the bathrooms, even enjoying it. This mom was in distress because she thought that cleaning the bathrooms should be a punishment.

Cleaning assignments are not punishments but are consequences a child receives for inappropriate behavior or behavior you want to change. If the child is whining, the applied consequences are designed to teach the child how to move out of a whining mood and move into a more productive attitude. The goal is to produce a vital, lively, emotionally mature, and happy human being who is not run by negative moods. In this case, a cleaning assignment worked very well since it snapped the child out of her mood.

12

Quick Reference - How Not to Engage Emotionally

A. Set boundaries in advance

B. Appreciate them; appreciate the brilliance of the game

C. Make them right

D. Respect a child's choices
(always give them two choices that work for you!)

E. Welcome mistakes (Edison learned from them)

F. Response versus reaction

G. Give immediate feedback –
be clear and precise and free of emotion

H. Apply Consequences

1. Natural
2. Designed (eg, arguing tree)
3. Agreed upon in advance (list with consequences)
  • Physical consequences like running or cleaning often
    work well

On the spot, call a team meeting

Peak Performance Trainings and Products:

Products: • Video tape
"*Rule #1: Mom Has Fun!*"

• Audio tape interview on
"*Responsive Parenting*"

Services offered: *Weekend and weeklong Seminar on:*
• Responsive Parenting
• Productive Relationships
• Self-actualization – The experience
• Private coaching
• Individual business coaching

To book Nicole MacKenzie for a teaching event, please contact:

Nue Nue Education
at MacKenzie International Consulting
Houston TX 77345

Office: 800-760-9425
Fax: 281-359-8924

www.micpeakperformance.com

About the Author

Nicole Iselin MacKenzie, a specialist in the field of human potential and peak performance, was born and raised in Zug, Switzerland where she obtained a degree in business and hotel-management. Nicole came to the United States in 1986 to study Maslow's theories of self-actualization and began to seriously pursue an education in the human potential field. As part of her education, she became a trainer in the Sage Learning Method and started "Curiosity Based" training in the United States as well as in Europe.

Nicole married in 1988 and had her first child in 1989. Holding her precious baby, Nicole realized that she knew absolutely nothing about raising children. Her daughter was born without instructions. All she knew was that she wanted to raise her child according to her new findings regarding the innate human potential. She became fascinated in finding methods to help parents maintain "curiosity" and vitality as well as a level of fun and satisfaction while raising their children and at the same time encouraging their children to develop unique, personal gifts as well as a highly developed emotional intelligence.

With this goal in mind, Nicole began her research on parenting techniques and developed the highly effective Responsive Parenting Techniques presented in this book.

Today, Nicole lives with her six children and her husband in Kingwood, Texas. She teaches classes internationally on how to establish a working relationship between parents and their children based on curiosity, fun, and peak performance.